W9-AQE-766

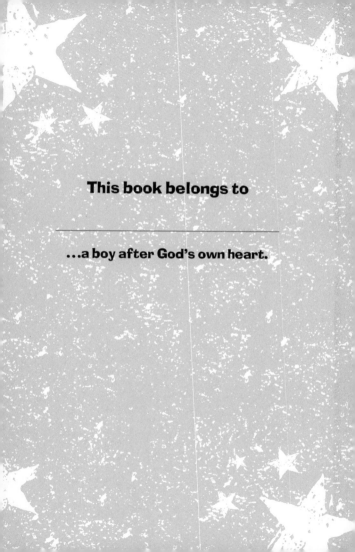

This book belongs to

_____

...a boy after God's own heart.

A BOY AFTER GOD'S OWN HEART

ACTION DEVOTIONAL

JIM GEORGE

HARVEST HOUSE PUBLISHERS
EUGENE, OREGON

Cover by Dugan Design Group

Cover photo © George Doyle / Stockbyte/ gettyimages

These devotions are adapted from *A Boy After God's Own Heart* by Jim George, copyright © 2012 by Jim George.

HARVEST KIDS is a registered trademark of The Hawkins Children's LLC. Harvest House Publishers, Inc., is the exclusive licensee of the federally registered trademark HARVEST KIDS.

A BOY AFTER GOD'S OWN HEART ACTION DEVOTIONAL
Copyright © 2017 Jim George
Published by Harvest House Publishers
Eugene, Oregon 97408
www.harvesthousepublishers.com

Library of Congress Cataloging-in-Publication Data
Names: George, Jim, 1943- author.
Title: A boy after God's own heart action devotional / Jim George.
Description: Eugene, Oregon : Harvest House Publishers, 2017.
Identifiers: LCCN 2016023936 (print) | LCCN 2016031833 (ebook)
    ISBN 9780736967518 (hardcover) | ISBN 9780736967525 (e-book)
Subjects: LCSH: Boys—Prayers and devotions. | Christian
    life—Meditations—Juvenile literature. | Boys—Religious life—Juvenile
    literature. | Boys—conduct of life—Juvenile literature.
Classification: LCC BV4541.3 .G452 2017 (print) | LCC BV4541.3 (ebook)
    DDC 242/.62—dc23
LC record available at https://lccn.loc.gov/2016023936

Printed in China

21 22 23 24 / RDS-CD / 10 9 8 7 6

Hey There!

I'm Jim. I'm so glad to meet you, and I think it's awesome that you're diving into this book of devotions. Our journey together is all about the most important adventure of your life—your adventure of living for God. Being a boy after God's own heart in today's world can be challenging and sometimes a struggle. But it's like that with anything that's worth going for!

As we get ready for our exciting trip together, I want you to know that I have you totally in mind as I write to *you*! I'm thinking about the things you're dealing with, the friends you're hanging out with, and the choices and decisions you're making. Everything that's big in your life. All the important stuff.

Your adventure with God is the most important adventure you will ever have. It's the experience of a lifetime. The biggest thrill in the universe. And the best thing about it? It leads you straight to God. God loves you. He loves you so much that He sent His precious and only Son, Jesus, to die for you on the cross so that you could know Him and live with Him forever.

So let's get into this! All it takes is a minute or two each day to learn more about God and how much He cares about you. You're valuable to Him. He has big dreams and huge plans for your life, and He's ready for you to discover them.

So—ready...set...here we go!

In Jesus' great and amazing love,

Jim George

Dream Big!

Do you ever dream about your future? Maybe you imagine yourself as an all-star professional athlete. Or a doctor who discovers the cure for a disease. Or a world-renowned explorer who dares to go where nobody has gone before. It's fun to dream big!

God wants you to dream about your future—and He wants you to dream big. That's because He has all sorts of plans for your life—people for you to meet, places for you to see, adventures for you to embark upon. With God, there are no boundaries. No limits. He loves to surprise you as He takes you on the ultimate journey to becoming a boy after His own heart. So never be afraid to set crazy goals and shoot for the moon. God wants you to go for it!

God, thank You for putting dreams in my heart and adventures in my life. Help me to stay focused on You as I discover what it means to be a boy after Your own heart. Don't allow me to settle for anything less than Your biggest and best dreams for my life. Amen.

Distracted

It's easy to get hooked on things you enjoy. A major example for almost every guy your age? Video games. Sure, they're fun and entertaining, but if you're not careful, they can totally eat up your time and distract your attention away from what's truly important. Like homework. Or eating dinner with your family. Or spending time with God.

Distractions like video games can give you a needed break from schoolwork or provide you with some downtime when you've been super busy. But be careful that you don't escape there too often. If you find yourself unable to stop thinking about playing video games or watching TV shows or doing anything else that takes your attention away from what you should be doing, stop right there. Talk to your mom or dad about setting limits on how much you play, and then get back to the things that are truly important!

Jesus, sometimes it's hard for me to stop playing video games or watching my favorite shows or escaping into my favorite books. Please help me not to get so distracted and not to let these things replace time with You or time with my family. Amen.

Focus

There's nothing wrong with fun distractions like video games or hanging out with your buddies or just goofing around. These things are just fine as long as you've taken care of your responsibilities. And as long as the fun stuff doesn't get too out of hand or go to extremes. The key here is keeping your focus on the big picture—knowing where the Lord wants you, as a guy of God, to focus your heart.

I know that talking about your heart isn't exactly a "guy thing," but hang in here with me. Jesus told all the people who wanted to follow Him, "Where your treasure is, there your heart will be also" (Matthew 6:21). He wanted them to think of the big picture—living a life that honors the Lord. So say a prayer to God and ask Him to work on your heart, and He'll show you where to focus your time and your attention.

Lord, it can be hard to keep my focus on what I need to do when my friends and my interests are pulling me in a bunch of different directions. Show me the big picture of what You want me to do with my life, and help guide my heart. Amen.

The Most Valuable Treasure

Your treasure is the thing that's most valuable to you. For some boys, it might be their favorite sport. For others, it's their desire to be part of the "in" crowd at school. And some guys might consider their best belongings their treasure—the coolest games, the trendiest shoes, the nicest ski equipment or skateboard.

That brings us to the biggest, most important question of all: Where is *your* treasure? Where's *your* focus? Where's *your* heart? A boy after God's own heart wants to make sure his treasure—what he thinks is most valuable and important in the whole world—is what God says it should be. Here's a hint: Your treasure shouldn't be about *you*. It should be about other people. And it should be about God. So go ahead and ask the Lord to lead you on a treasure hunt. It will be totally worth it!

God, thank You for directing me to the treasure You have for me. Help me to keep my mind and my heart always seeking treasure where You want me to find it. And please help me to make Your treasure my treasure. Amen.

Like a King

As you begin this awesome adventure in following Jesus and obeying Him, here's a key verse that shows you that God wants to be first in your life. It's Acts 13:22—and it's dynamite: "I have found David son of Jesse, a man after my own heart; He will do everything I want him to do."

In this verse God is describing the heart of the man He chose to be king over His people. God doesn't say the man had to be really smart or a super great athlete or the most popular guy around. He was concerned with one main thing—that the future king was *a man after God's own heart*. That should be the goal of your life too. That you'll be growing into a boy after God's own heart, a boy who follows God and is willing to go on the amazing journey of doing whatever God wants you to do.

Lord, I'm excited to begin the awesome adventure of becoming a guy after Your own heart. Thank You for giving me everything I need to begin this journey and for making me like a king if I follow You. Amen.

God's Great Love

Being a guy after God's own heart starts with realizing that He loves you. As much as your parents and grandparents love you, guess what? No one loves you more than God does. Let's look at what the Bible says about God's love.

- "God is love" (1 John 4:8).
- "God so loved the world [including you!] that he gave his one and only Son, that whoever believes in him shall not perish but have eternal life" (John 3:16).

It's totally hard to imagine that anyone could love you more than your mom or dad love you, but it's true. God loves you more than anyone ever could. After all, He sent His Son to die for you so you could have a place in heaven forever with Him. There's no way anyone could ever love you more!

God, I want to experience all the cool things You have for me. And the biggest and best of those things is Your incredible love for me. Thank You for sending Jesus to die for me so I can live with You forever. Help me to live for You as I experience Your love for me. Amen.

Commandments

What do you think of when you hear the word "commandment"? Some scary rule that's impossible to follow? An intense law that has major consequences if you break it?

It's actually pretty simple—and not freaky at all. A commandment is something God wants you to do. (It can also be something He *doesn't* want you to do.) And when you keep His commandments, He promises to bless you.

John 14:15 says, "If you love me, keep my commands." One key way to show your love for God is by doing what He wants you to do. And the things He wants you to do are *always* for your own good. When you choose to follow God's commandments, your thinking might go like this: *If God wants me to do this, I am going to do it. And if God doesn't want me to do this, I'm sure not going to do it!* Simple? Absolutely! Just love Him and follow His commandments.

Jesus, the words "obey" and "commandment" can sound pretty intense, but You've actually made things simple for me. As long as I keep talking to You and learning more about You, I'll understand better and better how to follow You. Amen.

How Can I Know?

It can be impossible to know something unless you ask! Have you ever wondered, "How can I know what God wants me to do? How can I be sure of what He wants?" Well, I have some great news for you! God has already told you His will in His Word, the Bible. He's already told you what He wants of you. So be sure to take some time every day to read your Bible.

And while you're reading your Bible, if something doesn't exactly make sense or you need more information, just ask your parents, your pastor, or your Sunday school teacher. God has put these people in your life to guide you and help you understand what He wants you to do, how He wants you to act, and the choices He wants you to make.

How can you know? You just need to ask!

God, when I'm having trouble figuring out the right thing to do or say, remind me that You have given me Your Word—the Bible—and that You have put people in my life to help me understand what You're telling me. Help me to ask when I'm stuck. Amen.

God's Flashlight

Have you ever been camping or hiking when your flashlight battery went dead and you were left totally in the dark? It's impossible to find your way when you can't see!

Did you know that God has given you a flashlight that helps you see when you're having trouble finding your way? Psalm 119:105 says, "Your word is a lamp for my feet, a light for my path." So if you have God's Word, you'll always be able to find your way.

And what about the times when you don't have your Bible right with you? That's when memorizing verses comes in handy. "I have hidden your word in my heart that I might not sin against you" (Psalm 119:11). How awesome is that? If you have access to God's Word—either in the pages of your Bible or in the depths of your heart—you'll always be able to find your way in the dark.

Lord, thank You for giving me the brightest light of all—Your Word—which I can use whenever I'm having trouble finding my way. Help me to memorize Your Word and keep it close to my heart so I won't get lost in the dark. Amen.

The Very Best Thing

What are the very best things in your life? Your family, right? And your friends. Probably also your pets. And hobbies like Legos or gaming. Or maybe some of the best things in your life are physical activities like baseball or swimming or soccer. And who can forget food—like ice cream, candy, and chips?

And never forget about God—He should be at the top of your "very best things" list. In fact, He wants you to love Him more than all other things. And He wants you to love Him with all your heart. The Bible says, "Love the Lord your God with all your heart and with all your soul and with all your mind" (Matthew 22:37).

Now, that's a lot of love—and even better than swimming and ice cream!

Jesus, when I think about the very best things in my life—my family, my friends, my favorite things to do—help me to remember that You should be at the very top of that list. Help me to love You more than anything else and to love You with all my heart.
Amen.

First

What does it mean to be first? It means you're the best. You're number one!

By now, you know that God should be the very first, number one thing in your life. But how do you put God first? It's not like you can make Him your top pick when choosing sides for baseball. But there are a few things you *can* do.

- When you go to bed at night, tell God that you love Him and that you are going to think about Him first thing as soon as you wake up.

- When you wake up, say "Good morning" to God and thank Him for His love, for His blessings, for all the good things in your life, and for a new day.

You'll never regret putting God first in your life.

God, help me to put You first in my life no matter where I go or whom I'm with or what I do. I want You to be the first thing I think about when I get up in the morning and the last thing I think about when I go to bed at night. Amen.

Write It Down

How good is your memory? If you're like most kids, you tend to forget things—sometimes a lot! Homework. Chores. Your mom's birthday. (Oops!) You're super busy, and it's totally normal not to remember everything. So what can you do to help you remember important stuff? You can write it down—on a sticky note, in your school notebook, even on the back of your hand.

If you haven't been doing it already, why not start writing down some things you don't want to forget? Especially things you learn about God and Jesus. You can also write down the things you're thankful for and the gifts God has given to you. Try it out! You'll be amazed at all you discover and learn when you just remember to write it down.

Jesus, sometimes I forget stuff. And sometimes I forget really important stuff. Help me to take note of the things I learn about You and all You do for me each and every day of my life. Amen.

Take Your Temperature

When you wake up feeling sick, what's one of the best ways to determine how sick you really are? You take your temperature. If the thermometer reads above normal—*boom!* You're staying home for the day. No school or sports or hang-out time with friends for you.

Did you know that your heart has a temperature too? The Bible talks about three heart temperatures.

- *A cold heart* doesn't even think about God—at all!

- *A lukewarm heart* is bored with God.

- *A hot heart* is on fire with love and enthusiasm for God.

So what's your heart's temperature? I hope it's burning for Him and ready to do all the awesome things He has planned for you. Because when it comes to your heart's temperature, hotter is better!

God, help me crank up the temperature of my heart so it's totally on fire for You. Give me the fiery heart of a guy who is completely committed to You in every part of my life. Amen.

Before He Knew You

Have you ever known all about someone before they even knew you? Of course not! Maybe you saw your best friend across the street kicking around a soccer ball when he first moved in and guessed that he was really into soccer, but you probably didn't know that his favorite kind of pizza was plain cheese or that his dog's name was Bandit.

God, though, has *always* known everything about you. He's known you through and through since before you were even born! And He loved you way before you first loved Him: "God demonstrates his own love for us in this: While we were still sinners, Christ died for us" (Romans 5:8).

That's one of those things that's both crazy and comforting all at the same time, isn't it? God loved you before you even existed in this world. That's some kind of love!

Lord, thank You that Your love for me has always existed and will always exist—no matter what. When I talk to You and tell You everything about my life, it's nice to know that You're a friend who has known me always and forever. Amen.

A Big Mess

Piles of wadded-up dirty clothes. A sea of T-shirts, socks, blue jeans, and gym clothes. Stacks of school papers, video games, and candy wrappers. Dirty carpet somewhere under there. And who knows what else!

Sound familiar? Sound like your room at times? (Or maybe all the time!) Why is it that we guys often like to live in chaos and messiness? Living in a sty may not bother you like it bothers your parents, but it can really mess up your life. Learning to organize your *stuff* gives you the skills for organizing your *life*. When you spend half an hour searching for your homework paper, that's half an hour less time to study. When it takes you 15 minutes to locate your basketball shoes, that's 15 minutes taken away from playing basketball with your brother.

So start taking care of your stuff. Put a few things away—and then a few more. The neater you keep your room, the better you'll feel. I promise!

God, my room is a mess. And when my room is a mess, it can make my life a mess when I lose things (and sometimes lose my temper!). Please help me to start being better organized about my space and my stuff. Amen.

Working Hard

Do you go off to work every day and bring home a big paycheck at the end of the month? Of course not! You're too young to be out in the working world (although the money would be nice, wouldn't it?). But just because you're too young to have an official job doesn't mean you're too young to have any responsibilities. This is the time of your life when you're becoming more and more mature and dependable, when you're learning what it means to work hard.

The Bible tells us, "Whatever you do, work at it with all your heart, as working for the Lord, not for human masters" (Colossians 3:23). What are some of those things you can work hard at? Helping out around the house. Studying. Practicing an instrument or a sport. Maybe even having a job that pays, like taking care of a neighbor's pets. Begin working hard now, and your efforts will definitely pay off!

Jesus, it's easy to slip into being lazy and assuming others will take care of stuff for me. Help me to start working hard right now so I can become someone who's dependable and responsible. Thank You for showing me the value of hard work. Amen.

Neat Freak

Experiments are cool, aren't they? You mix some stuff together and see what happens—often, it's something you never expected!

I have an experiment for you to try. Warning, though! It might have the crazy effect of shocking your whole family as well as your friends. Try being a "neat freak" for a few days and keeping your room clean. Make your bed. Vacuum your floor. Hang up your clothes. Put away your stuff. Then see what happens!

Here's a thought from God about being tidy and neat: "Everything should be done in…[an] orderly way" (1 Corinthians 14:40). This verse gives you a general principle for life, including the way you live and take care of your things. So give it a go. Become a neat freak for a day or a week and see what happens.

Lord, help me to try this experiment and get some order in my room and my life. And then show me what happens when I'm motivated to get stuff done and put things away. I know You don't expect perfection—which is a good thing!—but help me to always do my best. Amen.

Working Together

Have you ever thought it would be really cool to paint the walls of your room black? Or hang some strings of flashing lights on your walls? What about turning your room into a zoo with a whole bunch of animals—snakes and turtles and lizards?

While you want your room to be a reflection of yourself and your personality and the things you like, you also need to ask yourself a few more questions: Do the things in my room bring honor to God? And would my parents approve of everything in my room?

Here's another way to look at it. Suppose Jesus were to stop in and hang out in your room. Is there anything you would want to hide before He got there? If so, it probably shouldn't be there.

A pet snake is fine if your parents are okay with it. Posters on the walls are great if you think Jesus would approve. Keep it you, but also keep it good with God and good with your parents.

Jesus, my room is a reflection of who I am and what's in my heart. Let my space be a place where friends can hang out and get to know You and where I can feel comfortable living as a boy after Your own heart.
Amen.

He Knows You

It's a crazy, crazy concept. The God of the universe knows you. He really and truly *knows* you! Out of the more than seven billion people who live on this earth, He is totally interested in you and the things you do. He knows your likes and dislikes. The things that come easily to you and the stuff you struggle with. He knows what makes you sad and what makes you happy. He *knows* you.

That's what makes this adventure with Jesus so awesome. It's always best to travel with someone who "gets" you. It's nice to spend time with a friend you can just hang out with, whether you're talking or not.

When you're with Jesus, you can talk to Him. You can read His Word. You can write Him a note. Or you can just *be* in His presence. It might seem complex, but it's actually pretty simple. That's because He already knows you.

God, it seems so unbelievable that You actually know me and hear me and see me. Thank You that I always have Someone who understands me no matter what I'm dealing with. Amen.

Too Busy for Me

Have you ever felt like your family was too busy for you? Maybe your mom forgot to pick you up from track practice or your sister didn't have time to help you with your math or your dad never signed your field trip permission slip. When these things happen, it's easy to feel like you don't matter—and to get mad.

The main thing to understand is that your family really does love you, but sometimes stuff happens. Your mom's meeting runs late, and her text that she's on her way to pick you up doesn't go through. Your sister's teachers pile a massive load of homework on her, and there's no way she can help you. Your dad had to fix the windshield wipers on the car and totally forgot about the field trip. These things happen.

What can you do when you feel as if nobody has time for you? Remind yourself that *things happen*. People get busy. Family members forget. But they still love you—always. So pray for your family. Tell God all about how you're feeling. Ask for His help and then trust that He can—and will—work everything out.

Lord, it's hard to feel like anyone cares about me when everyone seems too busy to help me. Please remind me that I always matter to them and to You. Thank You for never being too busy for me. Amen.

God's Gifts

My parents are so stupid!" "My mom has no clue!" "My dad doesn't know anything!" Have you ever heard kids talk like this? Putting their parents down. Criticizing them. Making fun of them. Just being super negative.

If you listen too much to this kind of talk, you'll begin to think that's how you're supposed to talk about your parents. I heard a lot of this when I was growing up. And I still hear a lot of it now. But I remember the day I looked at James 1:17, which says, "Every good and perfect gift is from above, coming down from the Father." And then I realized something—those gifts included my parents!

God gave you your parents exactly the way they are and who they are. That means they are gifts from Him to you. This truth helps you see your parents as special gifts from God, just for you. And that's a positive thing!

Jesus, when other kids start saying bad things about their parents, help me to remember that my parents are good and perfect gifts from above. Thank You for giving me a family that loves me. Help me to love them in return. Amen.

Pray for Your Parents

Prayer is such a terrific habit. No matter what's going on in your life, you can always talk to God. He cares so much about you, and He wants to hear every little detail of your life. He also is interested in your relationship with other people, and He wants you to pray for them too.

Your parents are a super important part of your life, so it's natural that God wants you to pray for them. When you talk to God about someone and ask Him to love them and bless them, you'll start loving and caring about them even more.

A big part of praying is "always giving thanks to God the Father for everything" (Ephesians 5:20). So when you pray for your parents, be sure to thank God for them.

Lord, even though my family may not always seem perfect, I know that You put us all together for a reason. Help me to develop the habit of prayer and, as I do that, to pray and give thanks for my parents every single day. Amen.

A Different Way to Pray

Did you know that when you pray, you don't always have to do it by talking? In church and Sunday school, you're probably used to people praying out loud. And you're probably also familiar with praying quietly to yourself. But there are other ways to pray too. One of those is to write down your prayers.

All you need is a notebook or a journal or even just some pieces of paper stuck in your Bible. You can copy down prayers from the Bible. (Try looking in the book of Psalms for some amazing ones.) You can write down a list of things you're thankful for. You can put your prayer requests—big and small—on the page too. Or you can just write a letter to God, just as if you were writing a letter to your friend. It's all good! What's really fun is to look back at your prayer notebook or your letters to God and see how He answered you every time. Maybe in ways you didn't expect, but always in His awesome, perfect way.

God, when I get bored with praying out loud or praying silently, help me to change up the way I pray by writing down my prayers. Thank You for always listening to me and always answering me. Amen.

Growing in Gratitude

When you're really little, things just appear for you. Presents at Christmas. New clothes when you've outgrown your old ones. Toys that are just right for your age. As you get older, you realize these things don't just show up. Someone has to choose them for you and spend money buying them. That would be your parents. Or your grandparents. Or other relatives or family friends.

So whenever someone gives you something or does something for you—like cooks you a meal or washes your clothes or feeds your dog when you're away—be sure to say "thank you!"

You can start making a game of it. Choose a random number—three, ten, twenty-one—and thank God for that many things each and every day. And then be sure to express your gratitude out loud. As you grow in gratitude, you'll grow as a boy after God's own heart.

Jesus, it's so easy to take the people around me and the things they do for me for granted. So many people in our world forget to say "thank you." Help me not to be one of those people. Help me to express my gratitude. Amen.

That's the Rule

D o you ever wish there were such a thing as a world without rules? You could turn in your home-work—or not. You could run on the pool deck—or not. You could do your dishes—or not.

But sometimes we need rules in our lives.

Once your parents or teachers give you advice or make a rule or decision, it's important for you to do what they say. Let me give you a kind of scary example. One day right after I got my driver's license, I asked my dad if I could take the car out and ride around with some of my friends. My dad said no—he said I wasn't ready to go out on my own. Well, you guessed it. When he left for a business trip, I took the car out for a spin—and wrecked it.

My dad was definitely right! I wasn't ready to drive on my own, especially with a bunch of my friends. A world without rules might sound nice, but things are bound to go wrong. So listen to the rules and obey them with a happy heart.

God, sometimes it seems like there are so many rules for me to obey! Help me to see that these rules exist for my own good and keep me safe. Give me Your strength to obey them and do the right thing. Amen.

Learn to Respect

D o you show everyone in your life an equal amount of respect? Maybe. After all, you're a pretty good kid. But then again, maybe not. If you're like a lot of guys, you 100 percent obey your teacher at school, your football coach, or your summer camp counselor. But at home? When it comes to your parents? Well...

The thing is, why *wouldn't* you respect your parents just as much as someone who doesn't live in your house? Jesus has something to say about this: "Honor your father and mother" (Matthew 15:4). Pretty straightforward, huh? And Jesus isn't telling you to honor and respect them sometimes. He's talking all the time!

So, what exactly does it mean to respect your parents? It means you treat them politely. You admire them. You listen to them when they talk. You accept their decisions, follow their rules, and seek to please them. You treat them even better than you would treat your favorite teacher or coach. That's respect!

Lord, help me to treat the people in my home—like my parents—with just as much respect as I treat the people outside my home. Thank You for teaching me how to honor others, starting with my family. Amen.

What Do You Get?

When you give something, you usually get something, right? You give money to buy a new pair of sneakers. You give time studying for a test to get a good grade. You give up a Saturday with your friends to take care of your little brother and get paid (so you can buy the sneakers!). Now, I'm not saying the only reason to give something is to get something in return. That's just usually the way it works.

Did you know that God gives you something when you obey your parents? Ephesians 6:2-3 says, "Honor your father and mother...that it may go well with you." When you follow your parents' guidance and rules—when you *obey* them—God promises to give you something amazing and wonderful: "that it may go well with you."

Good stuff! There's a reward in obedience, in listening to your parents and taking their advice so that you make the right choices.

Jesus, thank You for giving me loving parents who help me make the right choices. It's so awesome that You have promised to bless me if I obey them and listen to them. Thank You for the rewards that come when I do the right thing. Amen.

Don't Be Mean

Do you know any guys who think it's cool to act like a jerk? These guys try to get big laughs by putting down a teacher. Or making fun of a classmate. Or just making rude comments about anyone they see walking down the street. And often, everyone else goes along with them. Not because the jerk is actually funny, but because they don't really know what else to do.

God wants you to love, honor, and respect people—no matter how dorky or how clueless they might seem. So be careful that *you're* not the one criticizing other people. And do take care to call out bad behavior. To stick up for the person who's being put down. To change the subject when the conversation starts getting negative and mean. Others will be relieved to move on. Including maybe even that jerky guy who started it all.

God, sometimes it's so easy to get caught up in being mean and making fun of people. Help me to remember that You would never treat others that way, and give me the courage to stick up for others when I need to. Amen.

Trust

Have you ever done a "trust fall"? A group of people stand behind you, and as you fall backward, they catch you and (hopefully!) keep you from hitting the ground. This might not sound like a big deal, but it is! You can't see the people behind you, and you can only hope that they're willing and able to catch you. That's trust.

It's not always easy to trust other people, but we can always trust God. The Bible says, "Trust in the LORD with all your heart and lean not on your own understanding; in all your ways submit to him, and he will make your paths straight" (Proverbs 3:5-6).

That's a powerful promise! When you follow God and choose to do what's right, He will show you the way to go. And His way is always the best way. So trust Him and then fall back—He's got this!

Jesus, it's so awesome that I can trust You no matter what. Even when I can't see what's going to happen, I know that You will always be there to catch me. Thank You for making it easy to trust You. Amen.

Love Ya!

It's an easy thing to say when you're headed out the door to school or crawling into bed at night: "Love ya, Mom!" "Love ya, Dad!" But saying "I love you" doesn't only have to be with your words.

You can say it with the things you do. The Bible says, "Dear children, let us not love with words or speech but with actions and in truth" (1 John 3:18). So besides saying the words "love ya," you can also show your love for others with your actions and by being truthful.

Unloading the dishwasher without being asked? That's showing love. Playing with your little sister so she doesn't cry? Love right there! Taking your dog for a walk? Yep, that's love! For those of us who have an easier time expressing love with actions than with words, this is good news. Love in action.

Lord, sometimes it's easy to say "I love you" with my words and sometimes with my actions. Thank You for giving us so many ways to share our love with others. And thank You for showing me that You love me. Amen.

Acting Out

Has someone ever hurt you—whether it's your brother punching your arm or a kid at school calling you names—and the next thing you wanted to do was hurt someone else? It can be a pretty natural response. Someone made us feel bad, so we want to pass on that hurt. It's almost as if passing on the hurt gets rid of our own hurt. But of course, that's not true. Hurting other people actually makes us feel worse, not better.

When you get mad and act out, you disappoint a lot of people. You disappoint your family and friends. You disappoint yourself. And you disappoint God. His plan is for you to turn to Him and the people who love you when you're hurting and upset. So next time someone hurts you, resist the urge to act out right away. Take a deep breath and ask God to help you hold it in. And not hurt someone else.

Jesus, when someone is mean to me, I sometimes want to hurt them right back. The world occasionally teaches us that this is fair and that we need to stand up for ourselves, but I know that You have a better plan. Help me to hand my hurt over to You. Amen.

Change of Heart

What do you do when you spill chocolate milk on your shirt or you get mud on your jeans? You change your clothes. Did you know that you can also change the way you feel and act? It's called having a change of heart.

The next time you're tempted to get angry or do something wrong, pray and ask God to help you change your heart. Tell Him what's been going on. Then ask for His forgiveness. Tell Him you're sorry about how you're acting—or how you're about to act—and ask for His help. And tell Him you want to follow His Word and do the right thing.

And then take the final step—do it! Make the changes you need to make. You can do it, because God will help you do it. Pray and work on having a happy, obedient heart in all things, and see what a radical difference having a change of heart makes.

Lord, I really need Your help on this one! Help me to change my heart when I feel like I'm about to really mess up. I know You're the one who can help me with my feelings and actions and responses. Thanks for always being there for me. Amen.

Royalty

Do you have a big sister who can be sooooo annoying? Or a little brother who can be such a pain? Although siblings can be super fun, they can also be super hard to live with sometimes. Like when your sister yells at you to leave her alone. Or when your brother won't leave *you* alone. You sometimes wonder, *Who are these crazy people I share a house with?*

Actually, did you know that your siblings are like royalty? At least, that's how you're supposed to treat them. Because your sister? She's a princess—a daughter of the King. And your brother? That's right, he's a prince—a son of the King.

Everyone is royalty—part of God's family. And as children of the King, we're supposed to serve each other. Honor each other. Love each other. So the next time you're having a tough go of it with your siblings, try to see them through God's eyes—as princesses and princes. Kids of the King.

> *God, it seems a little goofy to think of my siblings as princes and princesses! But You are the King, so it must be true. Help me to start seeing my siblings through Your eyes and giving them the honor and love to which they're entitled. Amen.*

Family First

Did you know that nothing is more special than a family? Over the years, your friends will come and go, but you'll always have your family. And believe it or not, the day will come when you and your brothers and sisters will actually get along with each other and want to spend lots of time together.

So start thinking now about that time together. When your sister isn't feeling well and wants you to watch a movie or play a game with her, say yes. When your brother needs an extra player for his pick-up basketball game, tell him yes. When you're having a family game night, jump right in even though you might want to be doing something else. You won't regret it.

As you grow up and get to make more and more decisions about what you do with your time, keep reminding yourself that family should come first.

Jesus, thank You for my awesome family! Help me remember that family comes first and that these are the people I'll know forever. Show me how to get along with them and have fun with them...even when I might feel like doing something else. Amen.

Loyalty

As a boy after God's own heart, you're probably not surprised that God should be your main priority. But after that, it's your family. And this means you need to make the decision to be true and loyal to your parents and your siblings.

If your parents need your help setting up for a garage sale, you need to be there instead of out skateboarding with your friend. If your sister has a big soccer playoff game, you should be there cheering her on instead of at home watching TV. If your brother has a piano recital, yep, you need to get dressed up and sit in the performance hall for a few hours instead of playing outside.

These things might seem like really big sacrifices at the time, but it's amazing how coming together and helping and supporting each other makes your family stronger. So be loyal!

Lord, it's easy to want to do my own thing instead of being there for my parents or my siblings. Help me remember that even though their activity might not be my favorite thing, the important thing is being loyal and true. Amen.

When Someone Is Hurting

A friend loves at all times, and a brother is born for a time of adversity" (Proverbs 17:17). Whom do you think the Bible is talking about in this verse? Actually, it's *you*! You're that friend and brother who is "born for a time of adversity." But what does that mean?

This verse is telling you how important family is when someone is suffering. Jesus wants you to be someone others can count on when they're sad or hurt or just having a hard day. You can do things for them or encourage them with your words. Sometimes just being there and hanging out with the hurting person is enough.

When things get tough, God is counting on you to be the friend and brother who is there for someone else. That's kind of cool to think that He—the awesome God of the universe—thinks so highly of you, isn't it?

Jesus, sometimes I don't know what to do when someone is hurt or is having a hard time. But in the Bible, You tell me that I'm an important part of making their life better. Help me to be a friend and brother others can count on. Amen.

Instead of Fighting

It's easy to fight with or yell at your brother or sister. It's easy to say mean things to them. And it's easy to call them names. But God wants something better from you. He wants you to pray instead of fighting or yelling.

It might be hard to understand, but praying for others changes you. And it changes your relationship with other people. Yes, praying for others can be hard—especially when they have hurt your feelings or ignored you. But go ahead and pray anyway. Ask God to help you love others no matter what. Ask Him to help you be kind, even when people are mean to you.

Here's a little secret: It's hard—impossible, really—to pray for others and hate them at the same time. When you pray, you'll discover you have a little more patience with people. And your feelings will turn to love and concern instead of anger and hatred.

Lord, please let my reaction to others be positive (praying) instead of negative (fighting and yelling). When I'm having a problem with someone, please remind me that the first thing I need to do is pray for them. And then help me know what to say or do next. Amen.

Enemies No More

It's a familiar theme in movies: the good guys versus the bad guys. But in real life, it's not clear who is good and who is bad. And that's why it's wise not to make enemies and assume that someone is not a good person.

The Bible says, "I tell you: Love your enemies and pray for those who persecute you" (Matthew 5:44). You might not be experiencing persecution the way some people do—like being locked up or starved or beaten. But when someone in your life makes fun of you for going to church or laughs at you for telling the truth, you're experiencing persecution.

You don't need to become best friends with that person, but you do need to take seriously what the Bible says to do. Love that person. And pray for them. You never know what could happen in their life. Because God loves both of you and can take care of any situation.

God, the last thing I want to do is pray for an enemy! But that's what Your Word tells me to do, so I know I need to obey You. Help me to see people the way You see them and to love them with Your love. Amen.

Control Your Tongue

Have you ever bitten your tongue when you were eating? It hurts, doesn't it?

Did you know that sometimes God *wants* you to bite your tongue? Not literally. But He does want you to bite back mean words or sarcastic comments that could hurt someone.

We all know what it's like to be on the receiving end of jokes, teasing, and name-calling. You can't control what others say and do, but you are totally in control of what *you* say and do! You can be mean and make fun of others—or not. You can laugh at others and put them down—or not. You can choose to control your tongue and keep your comments to yourself.

So the next time you feel tempted to tease your sister or talk back to your mom or make a rude comment to a classmate, stop! Bite your tongue and keep those angry words from spilling out. You'll be glad you did.

Jesus, I know I can't control what others say, but I can control the words that come out of my mouth. Help me to bite back mean words and comments when I feel them coming and to replace them with words of kindness. Amen.

Rules for Speaking

"Do not let any unwholesome talk come out of your mouths, but only what is helpful for building others up" (Ephesians 4:29). The Bible gives us some pretty clear rules for our mouths and what we say to others!

So what would qualify as "unwholesome" talk? Well, what about swear words? They usually make people feel uncomfortable. And rude comments and put-downs? Definitely unwholesome. Mumbling could also be considered disrespectful if you act like you don't care about the person you're talking to.

And about what you *are* supposed to say...that would be words that are "helpful for building others up." This would include sincere compliments. Words of encouragement. Even funny jokes and stories. (God created us with a sense of humor!) Just using a little bit of common sense, it's pretty easy to figure out the rules for speaking.

Lord, when I follow Your rules for speaking, I get along better with others and don't have as many problems. Help me to watch the words that come out of my mouth. Let me speak words that build others up.
Amen.

Attitude Adjustment

There's a scary story in the Old Testament about two brothers, Cain and Abel. Cain was angry with his brother because God liked Abel's offering better than Cain's offering. Listen in as God talked to Cain about his attitude: "The LORD said to Cain, 'Why are you angry?...Sin is crouching at your door; it desires to have you, but you must rule over it'" (Genesis 4:6-7).

Now here's the scary part. Cain didn't do what God said to do. He didn't adjust his attitude. Instead, "Cain attacked his brother Abel and killed him" (verse 8). Yikes!

God has a message for you here. The next time you get mad at a brother or sister, remember what God told Cain. And do what God told Cain to do—control your bad attitude before it controls you!

Jesus, this story about Cain and Abel is pretty freaky! But instead of letting it freak me out, help me use it to learn to adjust my attitude before something happens that I regret. Thank You for always helping me when I ask for Your guidance. Amen.

No Matter What

Have you ever decided you were going to do something—no matter what? Maybe it was jumping off the high dive. Or getting a good grade on your math test. Or making ten free throws in a row. It might have taken some time and effort and sacrifice, but you did it. No matter what.

There's something that God wants you to do no matter what. And He spells it out clearly in His Word: "A new command I give you: Love one another. As I have loved you, so you must love one another" (John 13:34).

That's God's version of no matter what. And it's hugely important! You're supposed to have a "no matter what" kind of love for your parents. For your brothers and sisters. For your grandparents. For your friends. It's the kind of love God wants you to have, a love that isn't based on other people's actions, a love that comes from God's love for you. No matter what.

God, thank You for giving me so much help in Your Word. No matter what's going on in my life and in the world around me, help me to love others. And thank You for loving me with the same kind of "no matter what" love. Amen.

Stick Together

Have you ever heard the saying, "Blood is thicker than water"? It means that your special, one-of-a-kind connection with your family (that's the "blood") is richer than your connection with other people (the "water"). And while you might not always get along perfectly, your family can come together like nothing else when things get hard. That's why it's so important to stick together.

The Bible says, "Be kind and compassionate to one another, forgiving each other, just as in Christ God forgave you" (Ephesians 4:32). This is a great verse to remember when you're having trouble forgiving your brother or you don't want to stand up for your sister. You need to remember to stick together and be there for each other, just like Jesus is always there for you.

When you choose to stick together and be there for each other, your family—with God's help—will have the strength to make it through anything.

Lord, sometimes I totally take my family for granted and forget how important we all are to each other. Help me to show them kindness and love even when it's hard. And remind me of the importance of sticking together. Amen.

Three or Four...or More!

Have you heard the motto of the Three Muske-teers? It's "All for one and one for all." In other words, we're all in this together! You might be a family of three or a family of thirteen, but one thing is the same—you're all in this together!

Live out this motto by helping make your home the best place possible for your family. If you're all in this together, you might as well make it good, right? And this starts with you being a son and a brother who is there for his parents and brothers and sisters. From there, you move on to thinking of others—putting their needs first and doing what's best for them.

Write your big brother a note of thanks for being a super sibling and slip it under his door. Play games with your little sister, hug her, and teach her things. Join your parents when they're making dinner or working in the garden. You're in this together—all for one and one for all!

God, no matter what size family I come from, we're all in this together. As my family works together to make our home the best possible place, remind us to always honor You. Amen.

An Only Who's Not Lonely

We've been talking a lot about getting along with brothers and sisters, but if you're an only child, don't worry—I haven't forgotten about you! Only children are super awesome, and God put you in your family for a very important reason.

Even if you don't have any siblings, you do have family members, friends, and lots of others you can consider brothers and sisters. So any advice about how to treat your siblings—like being kind to them, putting their needs first, being there for them—also applies to your cousins, friends, and everyone else.

As an only, it's important to make sure you don't get so caught up in your own world that you forget to think of others. Start imagining everyone as part of one big, happy family—a family you can love and serve. When you do that, you'll never be lonely!

Jesus, sometimes I like being an only child, but sometimes it can get pretty lonely. Thank You for putting people in my life—cousins, friends, neighbors—who can be like brothers and sisters to me. Help me to see other people as part of my "bigger family" and to show kindness and care to them. Amen.

Different Strengths

News flash: Nobody is good at everything! It might seem like it on days when your best friend scores the winning goal in the soccer game *and* gets the highest grade on the science test. Or when your little sister can finish a book in a day *and* rock her gymnastics meet. But nobody's perfect at everything.

Science might come easily to you, but spelling? Not a chance. Or you can play the drums like nobody's business, but you can't hit a baseball to save your life. And you know what? That's okay. God created people with different skills and talents.

If sometimes you feel like you're not as good as others, the best thing to do is to thank God for all the gifts He's given you. Because He *has* gifted you with strengths and abilities. And then ask Him to help you with your struggles. With God's help, you can always improve!

Lord, help me not to complain about the things I'm not good at and not to resent others for doing those things well. Remind me of the strengths and abilities You've put in me, and help me to use them to bring You glory and honor. Amen.

Boring!

Have you ever had a day or a week when you were totally bored with school? Even if you really like school and you're good at it, it's normal to occasionally get bored and feel like you'd rather be doing something else. Maybe math is hard this year. Or history is confusing with all those names and dates. And English seems like a waste of time because after all, don't you already speak English?

Sure, there's more to life than names and dates and math problems. But school is valuable because it teaches you some bigger life lessons. Like trying and trying until something makes sense. Or discovering you actually like something you thought you hated.

When you find yourself stuck in the rut of boredom, first pray about your attitude. Then try to find something interesting about the class. Pretty soon you'll be back on track and excited and ready to go, and the boredom will be a thing of the past.

Jesus, sometimes school is just so boring! I try to get interested in what I'm learning, but it just isn't happening. Help me to pay attention in class and to always do my best, even if I find the material totally boring. Amen.

Downtime

Your parents and teachers probably talk a lot about working hard and doing your best and plugging away at stuff. That's all important, but I have some news you're going to really like. It's also important to play hard and relax!

Sometimes, after studying super hard, all you want to do is kick back and relax with a snack and some downtime in front of the TV. Or ride bikes around the neighborhood with your buddies. Going for a hike in the woods with your dog works too. All of these things give your brain a break and help you come back to studying with more energy.

God created our bodies to work hard, but He also created them with a need for downtime. Some people in our world are so busy, they forget that they *need* time to relax and play and just hang out. So after you've worked hard, be sure to take some time to do something fun for yourself. God encourages it!

God, thank You for creating me to work hard as well as play hard. Help me to know when it's time to relax and when it's time to get back to studying or doing my chores. It's nice to know that I can always take a break when I need to. Amen.

Growing Up

I think all young guys look forward to being older, especially being old enough to drive a car! Maybe that's why we love birthdays—all those presents, and the bonus of being a little older and more grown up. (And being one year closer to driving that car!)

But with each year of growth comes more responsibility, like taking school more seriously or doing harder chores around the house or just becoming a more mature person. Those things can be hard, but they are important parts of growing up. They require dedication, commitment, and time.

Yes, growing up can be exciting and fun—more freedom, more friends, more challenges—but it can also be just plain difficult. That's why it's so nice to know that Jesus is with you every step of the way, including the first time you ride a bike and the first time you drive a car. He'll never give you more than you're ready to tackle, and He'll always be there for you.

Lord, most of the time, growing up is awesome! But sometimes I wish I didn't have all these chores or homework or expectations. Sometimes I just don't feel ready for them. Please help me to turn to You when I feel like I'm in over my head. Amen.

Life Lessons

D id you know that school teaches you way more than just the parts of speech, answers to story problems, or all the states and capitals? Whether you attend a public school, a private school, or home-school, school teaches you tons of life lessons.

You learn how to talk to and work with different types of people. You discover how to ask and answer questions, give reports and presentations, and talk in front of a group. You figure out how to find solutions to problems and challenges. You learn to act in a proper way toward those in authority and toward your peers. And being in school also teaches you to restrain your emotions—and your mouth!—and to focus your active mind and energy.

God is excited about all the life lessons you're learning as you journey through your education. Those things will help you grow into a guy after God's own heart!

God, please help me to remember that no matter where I am, You have life lessons for me to learn. Keep my eyes open so I pay attention and am able to grow from all of my experiences. Thank You for all of these awesome opportunities! Amen.

The Best Kind of Knowledge

What do you think is the most important subject in school? Is it science, so people can find cures for diseases and pathways to other planets? Maybe it's math because it's important to know how to measure and calculate. Foreign languages are pretty essential too, as people from other cultures need to learn to talk to each other.

The Bible tells us about the best kind of knowledge and where to find it. "If you look for [wisdom] as for silver and search for it as for hidden treasure, then you will understand the fear of the LORD and find the knowledge of God" (Proverbs 2:4-5).

Wow! God's knowledge *must* be valuable if it's compared to silver and hidden treasure. The terrific thing here is that His knowledge isn't hidden—it's right there in the Bible, ready for you to read and discover and possess. All you have to do is read your Bible and pray to receive the best knowledge of all.

Lord, thank You for making Your knowledge completely available to me. Help me develop the habits of reading my Bible and praying every day so I will learn all You have to teach me. Thank You for sharing Your wisdom with me. Amen.

Attitude Is Everything

Have you ever heard the saying, "Attitude is everything"? This saying can apply to a whole bunch of things in your life—school, chores, activities...even things like food and clothes! There are some things in life you can't decide for yourself—like how much homework your teacher assigns or what your mom cooks for dinner—but you *can* decide how you'll react to those things. You can freak out about the homework, or you can just plug away and get it done. You can complain about tonight's dinner, or you can eat it and look forward to having your favorite meal tomorrow.

When you choose to change your attitude, you can make things more fun and exciting, turning them into good memories. Or you can keep your old attitude and feel as if you're living a nightmare. *You* get to choose which it will be. Attitude is everything!

God, when I'm drowning in homework or stuck at home doing boring chores or choking down my least-favorite meal, it's hard to feel thankful! At times like this, help me to choose to have a positive attitude. Amen.

All There

I'd like to share one of my favorite quotes with you. It says, "Wherever you are, be all there."

"Well, of course!" you might be thinking. "If I'm somewhere, of course I'm going to be all there!"

True, you can't have your head at home while the rest of your body is at school. What I mean is that wherever you are—church, school, practice—make sure to pay attention to what's going on. Actively participate in the group discussion. Keep your head in the game.

There's a terrific verse from the Bible that shows what it means to "be all there." It's Colossians 3:23: "Whatever you do, work at it with all your heart, as working for the Lord, not for human masters." "With all your heart" means you put everything you have into what you're doing. It's being all there!

Jesus, when my mind starts to wander or when I feel like checking out, remind me that You want me to be all there. Help me keep my focus and my goals in mind as I learn to work with all my heart. And remind me that I'm ultimately doing it all for You. Amen.

Get Started

If you're like most guys I know, getting started on anything—writing a paper, doing 100 push-ups, cleaning out your closet—is by far the hardest part of any task. There seem to be so many things you'd rather be doing!

But you can't *finish* anything until you *start* doing it. God has a few hints on how we can get started on stuff—and with the right attitude. "Make every effort to add to your faith goodness; and to goodness, knowledge; and to knowledge, self-control; and to self-control, perseverance" (2 Peter 1:5-6).

Now, look back at the first three words of that verse. Make. Every. Effort. Sure sounds like giving yourself a great-big "get started" push, doesn't it? Getting stuff done requires something from you— effort and hard work! And the effort you make will pay off big-time as one good quality after another becomes a part of your life. So get started right away!

God, it's so hard to get started on something I don't want to do. I get distracted in a million different ways! But in Your Word, You tell me that I need to make every effort to get stuff done. Give me that push to get going and then to keep going. Amen.

Get It Together

School is a place for learning. But to learn well, you need to be organized. You'll never do well on your math test if you left your math book at school. Writing papers will be impossible if you can't find a sharpened pencil. And what about worksheets your teacher gives you? You'll need to keep those organized too.

Sounds overwhelming, huh? But little by little, you can get yourself organized. Start with your backpack. Go through it right now and get rid of all the stuff you don't need. You'll probably find stuff you'd forgotten, things you thought were lost. Bonus!

Then choose a good place to do your homework—the desk in your room, the dining room table, that little corner in the living room. Check with your family to see if that's a good place, and then do your homework there every time. Also make sure you have the supplies you need—sharpened pencils, erasers, plenty of paper. Once you've gotten things together, it's so much easier to get things done!

Jesus, it's so easy to let things get disorganized when I'm rushing out the door. Help me to become a more organized person so I don't waste time searching for stuff. Amen.

Make It a Game

When you're doing homework or chores, the time can drag on and on and on. The more you work, the farther away the finish seems. You thought you had to do 20 math problems—until you realized you were actually supposed to do 30. You thought you'd washed all the dishes—until you found those dirty plates and bowls in your room. (Oops!)

The best thing to do when you're feeling bogged down in work is to make it a game. Set a timer and try to beat the clock. Turn on some fun music (if you can concentrate while the music is playing). Do ten math problems, take a break and shoot ten baskets, and then tackle ten more problems.

Hard work doesn't have to be dull and boring—it can be fun! So choose to make it a game and see how much you can get accomplished.

God, thank You for creating a world full of music and creativity and imagination. Help me to use these tools when I'm feeling like I'll never get my homework or my chores done. Thank You for being such an awesomely creative Creator! Amen.

Sooner Is Better

Do you want to know a major secret to being successful in anything? Sooner is better. Don't put things off and say you'll do them in an hour or tomorrow. If you have the time, do them right away!

The smart guys (not IQ smart, but smart with their time) do some of their homework while they're at the bus stop. Or while they're waiting on the steps at school for their ride home. Or while they're at their grandmother's house and Mom is on her way home from work. Whatever works best for you, make that your time to get things done. Then, after you're done, you can play games, watch TV, or go outside to play ball.

Homework and chores aren't the only things you can put off. It's also easy to put off spending time with God. That's another case where sooner is better. Make it a point to talk to God first thing in the morning, to read a devotional or a few Bible verses to help you with your day. Sooner is always better!

Jesus, it's super easy to be lazy and put off doing homework, chores, or even time with You. Help me to remember that sooner is better and that when I get things done right away, I don't get stressed. Amen.

Just Do It

I've been able to do a lot of things in my life. I'm a pharmacist, a soldier, a pastor, a missionary, a teacher, and a writer. How did all of this happen? Definitely not by daydreaming about things I'd like to do someday. I had to just do it!

Take writing books. Every day over the years, I've gone to my desk (my place where all my favorite things are) at a certain time. I stay there until I've written five pages.

When I was a kid doing my homework every day, I learned *how* to get things done. And I can tell you that years and years—and years!—of doing homework in a certain place at a certain time prepared me for all the jobs I've been able to do. God has special work for you as well, and He'll show you how to get it all done if you promise to show up and just do it.

God, You have a lot for me to accomplish, and I just need to show up and do it. Thank You for building good habits in me as I learn how to get things done.
Amen.

Find Your "Thing"

Have you ever felt like you have no idea what your "thing" is—the activity or skill that seems to be the perfect fit for you? Maybe your brother is a math whiz and your sister already has her black belt in karate and your best friend can play the trumpet like a pro. But you? No clue!

That's okay. This is the time in your life when you can try out a lot of different activities without feeling a bunch of pressure to be perfect at just one thing. Some kids *do* find their "thing" early. For others, it takes longer. And that's okay.

Even Jesus had to learn and grow! "Jesus grew in wisdom and stature, and in favor with God and man" (Luke 2:52). It didn't happen suddenly for Jesus, and it doesn't have to happen suddenly for you. You'll get there eventually. You'll find your "thing." And until then, keep learning and growing and having fun!

Lord, sometimes it feels like everyone has it all fig-ured out—except me! I know I need to be patient and that I have a ton of learning and growing to do. Thank You for putting people in my life to encourage me and to help me find my "thing." Amen.

Ask About It

D o you love to read stories or watch movies about life long ago? It's so cool to imagine what it would be like to sail with one of the great explorers or to be a cowboy in the wild West.

You have an awesome source of stories in your own family! Sure, your parents and grandparents weren't ancient Greeks or Romans. (They aren't *that* old!) But they do have some pretty amazing stories to tell if you would only ask them.

Your parents and grandparents know all about what it was like being a kid—and times were different for them. It's super fascinating to hear about the discipline, the effort, and the hard work of their childhood—as well as all the fun and crazy things they did. So go ahead and ask them about what life was like when they were your age. And ask them how they came to know and love Jesus. Their stories might just be better than any book or movie!

God, sometimes I forget that some of my best learn-ing resources are right in my own family. My parents and grandparents can share their stories and help me grow as a boy after Your own heart. Thank You for blessing me with them. Amen.

Old School

If you really want to go old school in learning about the past, head for the pages of your Bible. You might think those stories don't really apply to a boy growing up in today's world, but they totally do!

Do you want to learn about having courage to do the right thing? That's in the Bible. The power of friendship? That's there too. Staying strong when everything around you is falling apart (sometimes literally)? Yep, in the Bible.

God uses the gift of stories—stories from the lives of real people—to help us learn more about Him. What His character is like. How much He loves us. How He longs to guide us and challenge us. So go ahead and jump into the stories—they have plenty of action and adventure and drama. Then pray and ask God what He would have you learn and discover from them.

Lord, it's easy to feel like I wouldn't be able to relate to stories that happened so long ago. But You gave us the Bible as a guide for our lives today—no matter when we're living on this earth. Help me to discover all You would have me learn through Your Word. Amen.

Listening More Than Talking

It's a well-documented fact that you learn the most when you listen more than you talk. That can be hard though. We all have stuff to say, and it's fun to be a part of the conversation. But make sure that you listen and try to remember what you heard.

The Bible says, "Let the wise listen and add to their learning" (Proverbs 1:5). What do smart people do? They listen! And then they apply what they learned to their lives. When you listen intently, some things might not make sense. And that's when you need to talk—to ask questions, to clarify, to understand.

You can listen to your parents and teachers and coaches and gain wisdom from them. You can listen to your friends. You can also listen to God when you read the Bible and pray. Sure, you can always talk, and you *should* contribute to conversations. But make sure you're listening as well—and then add to your learning.

God, it can be really hard to listen, especially when I feel restless or bored. But You have so much for me to learn—in the classroom, in Sunday school, at home...Help me to keep my mouth shut when I need to and to live out what I learn. Amen.

What's Most Important

We've been talking a lot about school. And friends. And family. As important as those things are in your life, there's something that's even more important. That's your relationship with Jesus.

As a boy after God's own heart, your relationship with your Creator is *the* most important thing of all. So along with homework, music practice, sports competitions, household chores, and everything else going on, be sure you're also taking care of your walk with Jesus. That's because "the LORD gives wisdom; from his mouth come knowledge and understanding" (Proverbs 2:6).

When your walk with the Lord is strong, everything else just kind of falls into place. This doesn't mean everything will be easy and perfect, but it will be better. You'll feel less stressed and more at peace. You'll be able to focus on what's important, and God will be right there with you.

Jesus, things can get pretty crazy in my life! Please remind me to make sure my walk with You is my number one priority as a boy after Your own heart. I know that other things are really important, but the main thing in my life is following You. Amen.

Friendship Failure

Have you ever had a best friend who was just like you? You and this friend did *everything* together. You were inseparable—until the day that other kid moved in down the street.

Maybe the new kid was a little older and had a little more stuff and just seemed a little cooler. Whatever it was, your best friend was suddenly always doing things with the new kid. And you were left out.

Ouch! That can really hurt. It can also be a problem if *you're* the one hanging out with the new kid and leaving out your best friend. Whatever happened, it was definitely a friendship failure. And this is something that makes God pretty sad. He created us to be friends with each other and to worship Him together. But because we're human, that doesn't always happen. God gets it though. And that's why you can always turn to Him when you find yourself in a hard place with your friends.

Lord, it can be really confusing when my friendships change and when I don't know who is my friend anymore. I don't like to feel left out, and I don't like how I feel when I leave others out. Show me how to be a good friend to everyone around me. Amen.

Finding Good Friends

riends. Sometimes it seems like you can't live with them, and it sure seems like you can't live without them! They are definitely an important part of your life, aren't they?

So be careful when and how you choose your friends. Your goal is to choose friends who help you to grow into a guy after God's own heart. And at the same time, you need to be a true and real friend to others. When you're hanging out with someone, try to determine whether Jesus would approve of this friend. How he speaks. How he acts. How he treats others. And also try to determine whether God would approve of the way *you* act when you're with this friend. God wants you to have great friends—and friends who follow Him are the best friends of all!

Jesus, I know that surrounding myself with good friends who also follow You is super important. My friends have a big influence on me, so I want them to be the right kind of people. Please put friends in my life who are good to hang out with and who help me be a better person. Amen.

Sticking Together

When I was about your age I had a best friend who lived just down the street from me. We liked the same things and were always together. But then, when we went into middle school, we were no longer in the same classes. That meant we had to work hard to remain friends.

What did we do? We made sure to meet during lunch break. And we went to each other's house often. During the summer we signed up for the same baseball league. We did all we could to remain close friends.

It's the same way with Jesus. Sometimes you find yourself falling away from His friendship. You get busy and forget to read your Bible. You go to sleep at night, forgetting to pray. The awesome thing is that Jesus is never too busy for you. He'll always have time for you, which means your friendship with Him is secure.

God, friendship can take some work! When I feel like a good friend is drifting away, help me to keep our connection strong. Most of all, help me to keep my connection with You strong. Thank You for never drifting away from me. Amen.

A True Friend

If you were to write down all your favorite things about your best friend, what would you say? Maybe that he's really funny. Or that he's good at martial arts. Or that you like the same kinds of foods. Or that he's never mean to you.

The Bible tells us the best thing about a true friend. "A friend loves at all times, and a brother is born for a time of adversity" (Proverbs 17:17). Sure, laughing and having good times together are parts of a solid friendship. But the most important quality of a friend is that he's there for you all the time. You want to hang out with people who are loving and kind—not mean and aggressive. You also want your friends to stick with you when you're in trouble or when you're having a hard time. Friendship is a good thing, and friendship based on the Word of God is the best friendship of all!

Lord, sometimes I look at the outward things in a friend—how cool he is, how talented he is, how popular he is. But You remind me that the inward things are more important—like kindness and compassion. Help me remember this as I make friends. Amen.

No Cliques

A clique might sound more like a girl thing, but did you know that guys can have cliques too? Sometimes a squad of guys can leave others out even more than a group of girls! You can recognize a clique when you see a group of people who spend all their time together and don't allow others to join them.

There's nothing wrong with having a group of friends who are similar to you. But it becomes a problem when the group acts mean and exclusive and leaves others out. Is that the kind of group you want to be part of? I don't think so. Everybody is a *somebody* to Jesus. Everybody deserves to be included. Open up your circle of friends and invite others in. After all, that's what Jesus did for all of us!

God, it's easy to hang out with people who are just like me. But it's also easy to let a clique form and to leave others out. Even though I might feel uncomfortable hanging out with people who are different from me, help me to see and accept others as You see and accept them. Amen.

A Friend to All

Jesus was a friend to everyone—and I mean *everyone*! Happy people, sad people. Well people, sick people. Rich people, poor people. He was even a friend of "sinners" (Luke 7:34). He was even criticized because He ate and drank and talked with the "wrong" people—people who were rejected by others.

It takes a lot of bravery and courage, but if you want to be like Jesus, you need to befriend the "wrong" people. I don't mean you need to join in the behavior of a group that makes wrong choices. But you *do* need to see people through Jesus' eyes and treat them the way He would treat them. That boy who always eats lunch alone? Find a spot at his table and eat lunch with him. The kid with the learning challenge who acts up in class? See if he needs help with his homework. Be like Jesus. Be a friend to everyone.

Lord, show me the people in my life who need a real friend and the people who need to know You. Help me to invite these people to church activities, where they can meet mature Christians and discover more about You. Give me courage to be a friend to everyone. Amen.

The Strongest Friendship

The strongest friendship in your life isn't going to be with your favorite soccer buddy or your best friend since way back in preschool or even your brother. Those are definitely friendships worth holding on to, but they won't be your strongest friendship. That's because the most important relationship in your life will be your friendship with Jesus.

Keeping your relationship with Christ strong helps you in so many other ways. When that friendship is strong, you don't mind the cliques or being left out as much. You'll also attract other friends who want to be more like Jesus. They might even ask you questions about why you seem different—why you're not mean, why you don't make fun of people, why you're so accepting of others. And when you answer, you can point them right to Jesus. You can tell them how your strongest friendship can be their strongest friendship too.

God, help me to know that my strongest friendship is my friendship with You. This is the foundation of all my other friendships. Thank You for always being my best friend. Amen.

Being Different

You've probably noticed that some kids are just different from others. Maybe they have a form of autism that makes it hard for them to act the right way in social situations. Or a learning challenge that makes school super hard. Or a physical challenge that prevents them from participating in a lot of activities.

Or maybe *you're* that kid who is a little bit different. I'm here to tell you that it's okay to be different from most people. Jesus certainly was. The words He spoke and the way He lived His life were totally unlike what people were used to. But look at all He accomplished! He stayed true to His Father and followed His plan. He was different, but He made a difference!

Often, the people who are different from others can make the biggest difference. So try not to worry if you have friends who are different from you or if you yourself are seen as different. That's just the way God made you, and He has an awesome plan for you.

Jesus, it's hard to be different. And it's hard to have friends who are different. But I know that You made us just the way we are. Help me to accept myself and to accept others as I do my best to make a difference for You. Amen.

Be Careful

Who are you? And who do you want to be? Ask yourself these two questions as you look for friends. And then choose those friends wisely. Why? Because you become what they are. The Bible is super clear when it tells you what to look for in a friend—and what to avoid at all costs. Your first goal is to seek out friends who are going in the right direction—toward Jesus. You should look for guys who will pull you along on your journey with Jesus. Where will you find friends like this? Usually you'll find them at church or in Christian groups or activities.

The Bible says, "Walk with the wise and become wise, for a companion of fools suffers harm" (Proverbs 13:20). So look for friends who are wise and not foolish—not necessarily straight-A smart, but those who make smart choices. Be careful when you choose your friends.

God, if my friends are wise, I will become wise. And if my friends are foolish, I will become foolish. The Bible makes this pretty clear! Help me to choose my friendships carefully because that will have a huge effect on who I turn out to be. Amen.

The Ten Commandments of Friendship

Here are ten ways you can be the kind of person who makes friends easily.

1. Speak to people—nothing is as nice as a cheerful word of greeting.

2. Smile at people—it takes 72 muscles to frown and only 14 to smile!

3. Call people by name—the sweetest music to anyone's ear is the sound of their own name.

4. Be friendly and helpful—if you want to have friends, be friendly.

5. Be cordial—speak and act as if everything you do were a real pleasure.

6. Be genuinely interested in people—you can like *everyone* if you try.

7. Be generous with praise—cautious with criticism.

8. Be considerate of the feelings of others—it will be appreciated.

9. Be thoughtful of the opinions of others—respect their right to think for themselves.

10. Be alert to serve people—what counts most in life is what we do for others!

Lord, help me to live by these ten commandments of friendship. When I'm unsure what to say to someone or how to act around someone, remind me that You've already let me know what to do. Amen.

The Golden Rule

retty much everyone has heard the Golden Rule. "Do unto others as you would have them do unto you." Who do you think made that up? Your parents? Nope, even though they might say it all the time! It was even popular before Jesus taught it in Luke 6:31. Jesus knew the world would be a much better place if everyone followed that instruction.

The Golden Rule tells us one reason to treat others well—so they will treat us well. This is more than just being nice. The apostle Paul wrote, "Be kind and compassionate to one another" (Ephesians 4:32). When you show kindness, you put others first. When you show compassion, you put yourself in another person's shoes and imagine what life is like for them—and then you act on what you feel.

So don't just be a little bit nice so others won't be mean to you. Be *a lot* nice—be kind and compassionate as you follow the Golden Rule.

God, You knew that the world would work a lot better if everyone put the Golden Rule into practice. Help me to show others kindness and compassion—and to treat others the way You treat me. Amen.

Kindness Counts

Isn't being nice enough? What is the difference between being nice, and being kind and compassionate? When you're nice, you're polite. You aren't mean. Being nice is just fine—it's great, actually—but it's best to go a step beyond nice.

Being kind is being thoughtful and really caring about someone. And being compassionate is really feeling what they are feeling and acting according to those feelings. Ask yourself, *What would be best for them? What would they like? What do they need me to say or do?*

As you probably know, you can act nice toward someone even when you really can't stand them. But you can't fake kindness or compassion. Those are sincere actions that come from your heart. And when it comes to having a heart that follows God, kindness and compassion are part of the plan.

Jesus, maybe I can fake being nice, but there's no way I can fake kindness or compassion. Give me a heart that is open to others and lets me see life from their point of view. Amen.

Keep It Secret

The thing that most people find easiest to talk about is other people. It's fun to tell stories about crazy things your friends or family did, but make sure you don't veer into the danger zone of telling secrets or spreading rumors. Before you tell a story or make a comment about someone else, ask yourself, *Should I be keeping this secret? Is this going to make the person I'm talking about look bad?* If the answer is yes, don't say it!

The Bible teaches that a true friend is loyal and knows how to keep a secret.

- "Whoever spreads slander is a fool" (Proverbs 10:18 NKJV).

- "A talebearer reveals secrets, but he who is of a faithful spirit conceals a matter" (Proverbs 11:13 NKJV).

It's also important not to *listen* to gossip. If someone says, "I'm not supposed to say anything about this, but..."—stop them! Tell them you aren't interested. Remember, Jesus wants you to be a friend to others. And part of that is knowing when to keep things secret.

God, sometimes I have trouble telling the difference between funny stories, secrets, and rumors. Help me to discern the difference between them and to remain silent when I should. Amen.

Share Jesus

It's awesome to share stuff with your friends—offering someone a piece of your favorite pizza, helping them with homework, or loaning them your baseball glove. But the best thing to share with your friends is the good news of Jesus.

Sharing Jesus might sound a little weird—how do you share a person, especially someone you can't see? But it's actually pretty easy to share Jesus with your friends. The best thing to do is to stay connected to Him—read your Bible, pray, and ask for opportunities to tell your friends about Him. Then try to live like Jesus so your friends see what it means to be His follower. You can also invite them to Sunday school or church activities. And definitely pray for your friends!

Jesus is the truest friend you could ever have and will ever have (John 15:15). Because He's the best friend any guy could ever have, you want to tell others about Him, right?

Jesus, You're the best friend I could ever hope to have. You mean so much to me, and I want my friends to know You too. Help me to live my life for You so that others can see You in me. And give me the courage to tell my friends about You. Amen.

Start with Prayer

You may have a ton of friends, or you might be trying to find more friends. Either way, it's important to keep praying about your friendships. The older you get, the more your friends will influence who you are and who you become. The right friends will help you make good choices, and you can be there for each other when things get tough.

What can the right friend do for you? He can encourage you in the Lord. He will challenge you to grow spiritually and continue on your adventure with Jesus. In fact, he'll be right there by your side, enjoying your journey with Jesus together with you. And he will stay with you even when things get really hard. How awesome is that!

So as you look for a good friend, start with prayer. And whatever you pray, always say it from your heart.

Lord, please bring friends into my life who will encourage me and stand by me. Give me wisdom and patience as I look for true friends. And help me to be the kind of friend to others that I would want to have for myself. Amen.

Get Pumped

What a week! Up for school early Monday through Friday, and then up super early for a soccer tournament on Saturday. Plus you went to bed super late every night. Wouldn't it be nice to sleep in just *one* day of the week?

Sometimes it's hard to get up for church on Sunday, but it's so worth it! Sunday is when you can get together with other believers and worship God, learn about Jesus, and hang out with others who can encourage you in your walk with the Lord.

So get pumped for Sunday! Set your alarm, haul yourself out of bed, and turn on some energetic music to get you going. And even if you're tired, resist the urge to argue or complain about getting up and getting ready to go. Sunday is the best day, and it sets the tone for the rest of your week. Get pumped!

God, sometimes I just want to sleep in on Sunday morning. For some reason, it's super easy to be grumpy and have a bad attitude, even when I know the best place for me to be is in church. Help me to get pumped about learning more about You. Amen.

Where Is Church?

When you hear the word "church," what do you think of? A fancy brick building with wooden pews and stained glass? Or a brand-new, up-to-date space with spotlights and cool music and casual chairs?

In the Old Testament, God asked His people to worship Him in a specific place—first a tabernacle (a portable tent) and then a temple (a building in Jerusalem). But in the New Testament, God built His church out of people. So the church is not a building. It's a group of people who believe in Jesus as their Lord. And this group of people is incredibly important to God! The Bible says, "Christ loved the church and gave himself up for her" (Ephesians 5:25).

God doesn't care *where* you meet and worship Him. It can be in an ornate cathedral or at a campsite in the woods. No matter where you are, He promises to show up. He'll always be there!

Jesus, thank You for making people more important than things. That's the way it is with the church—You care more that we meet than where we meet. Let me focus on the people and on You when I'm worshipping. Amen.

How to Worship

Is church a place where you're supposed to be quiet and try not to fall asleep during the songs or sermon? No way! Church is supposed to be fun and the absolute best part of your week. So when you head to church, go with a positive attitude.

When you get there, pay attention. If there's discussion time, share and ask questions. This makes the message a lot more real to your life. And always be friendly, leaving open the possibility of making new friends.

The Bible tells us, "Worship the LORD with gladness; come before him with joyful songs...Enter his gates with thanksgiving and his courts with praise; give thanks to him and praise his name" (Psalm 100:2,4). That sure doesn't sound like a place to take a nap. When you go to church with an eager and open heart, you grow—and you please God with your worship.

God, sometimes I feel like church is boring and dull, but You say it's not supposed to be like that! Help me to head for church with a positive attitude and to listen, learn, speak up, and make new friends. Amen.

Get Involved!

Church is a special place God provided for His people—those who love Him—to get together. And there are so many ways to get involved!

Most churches have Bible clubs where you can play games, memorize Scripture, talk about Jesus, and have fun with other kids your age. I loved our church's annual summer camp. It was next to a big lake and had a gigantic swimming pool that was so much fun on hot summer afternoons. Best of all, I liked gathering together with the youth leader and the other kids to talk about the most important person in the world—Jesus!

Try not to miss out on these church activities. The things you do and learn, and the commitments you make during these times, can be some of the most important and memorable ones of your entire life. Plus, you can begin some great, for-real friendships with other boys who follow Jesus too.

Lord, sometimes it's hard to jump into new things and get involved, but it's totally worth it! Thank You for awesome opportunities, like Bible clubs and summer camps, where I can learn more about You. Please help me make these activities a priority in my life. Amen.

A Quiet Place

There's a story in the Bible about a special time Jesus spent with His disciples. He told them, "Come with me by yourselves to a quiet place" (Mark 6:31). Jesus spent tons and tons of time with big crowds, but He also understood the importance of time alone with the Father.

Where do you feel close to God? For some boys, it's out in nature, praying and talking to God. For others, it's hanging out in their room listening to music and reading their Bible. It doesn't really matter *where* you go to hang out with God, but it does matter that you take time to talk to Him and tell Him what's going on in your life.

So be like the disciples and get away to that quiet place. You can hang out with God for five minutes or five hours. The place and time don't matter as much as actually doing it. Find your quiet place and invite God to join you.

God, it's fun to hang out with friends and do stuff with big groups, but I also grow from spending time alone with You. Help me to find my special place and make time for You on a regular basis. I know You will always meet me there. Amen.

All the Same

Imagine everyone being exactly the same—that wouldn't be very interesting, would it? God created every person as a unique individual. But there's one way we're all the same—God loves each and every one of us equally with His amazing love.

One of my favorite sayings is, "The ground is level at the foot of the cross." This means we're all the same when it comes to having a relationship with Jesus. In Christ, we are all one. Galatians 3:28 says, "There is neither Jew nor Gentile, neither slave nor free, nor is there male and female, for you are all one in Christ Jesus."

So celebrate your differences and what makes you and your friends unique, but realize that God loves each and every person with the same amazing love. He doesn't love some people more than others or think more highly of certain people. He loves equally!

Jesus, I'm glad I don't have to do anything to earn Your love or to make You love me more. It's nice to know that even though You have created people with so many differences, Your love is the same for each of us. Help me to love others as You love me. Amen.

Reach Out

You may not be a pastor or a youth leader, but did you know that as a follower of Jesus, you have a ministry in your church? Jesus expects all His followers to reach out to others. And don't worry—these acts of friendliness are easy to do.

- Say hi to everyone—and smile.
- Sit by any boy who is alone. If you are with a friend, you can both go sit with him.
- If someone is new or a visitor, be sure to say hello and get to know him.

When others see you being friendly and reaching out, they'll start acting that way too. And pretty soon you have a big group of people who are including everyone, having fun, and living for Jesus together. So take that first step and reach out!

Lord, the hardest part of anything can be taking that first step and doing it. That definitely includes reaching out to others. Help me to see everyone as a potential friend and to set a good example of being welcoming and inclusive. Amen.

It's All About Jesus

Music and activities and sermons are all part of church, but they aren't what church is all about. Church is all about one thing—Jesus. The focus on Him is what makes church special. You go there to learn about Him. You connect with others who are doing their best to live for Him. The focus of church is Jesus.

So listen up when you're in Sunday school or sitting in on the sermon. Discover more about Jesus and His amazing life and miracles. Hear about His love and character qualities. You'll be blown away as you learn about what Jesus has done for you—that He died for you and your sin.

Even if the music at your church is boring or your best friends are away on vacation, those things shouldn't really matter. Church isn't about the building or the people or the music—it's about Jesus. And that's enough to make it more than worth your time!

God, when I complain about certain things in church,
help me to remember that those things aren't as
important as You and Your love for me. Keep my
focus on You. Amen.

Decision Time

The most important decision you will ever make in your life is whether you will follow Jesus and give Him your heart and life. This is the biggest decision of your entire life—way more than where you go to college or what career you pursue or whom you marry. And unlike those decisions, it's a decision you can make right now!

Jesus invites us to come to Him (Matthew 11:28). If you haven't already made the decision to come to Him, I'm praying that God will use His Word to open your heart to the truth of His love for you and that you will respond to His invitation.

When you give your heart and your life to Jesus, you've made the best decision you could ever make. You've chosen the path God has planned for you, and you'll be able to live your entire life as a guy after God's own heart.

Jesus, if I haven't already made a decision to come to You and follow You, please open my heart to accept Your love and Your Word. This decision is a huge step for me—one that will affect the rest of my life. Thank You that I can come to You at any time. Amen.

Who Jesus Is

When you make the decision to follow Jesus, one of the best things to do is learn who Jesus is. It's easy to come to know Him, but learning about Him and how to follow Him is something you do for the rest of your life. That's because there's always more and more to learn about Him.

In the Bible, Jesus says, "I am the way and the truth and the life. No one comes to the Father except through me" (John 14:6). In other words, He's the only path to God. You don't gain a place in heaven by doing good works or putting a certain amount of money in the offering or becoming successful. You get there by believing in Jesus.

Basically, Jesus is *everything*. He should be everything to us here on earth, and He's the One whom we long to be with someday in heaven.

Lord, I long to get to know You and to become more and more like You. I want to spend my whole life learning about You, but I can also know You and follow You right now. Thank You for being the path to the Father. Amen.

Help Out

The church is sometimes called the body of Christ. People in the body of Christ help each other—and you can help others too! If you're having a bake sale to help raise money for kids to go to church camp, ask your mom if she can help you bake some cookies. If teachers need help setting up a classroom, ask your parents if it's okay to show up a little early to help out.

You can also help your parents with their ministries. I know a mom and dad who volunteer to take care of the babies in the church nursery—and their kids gladly help them after church is over. Their son Jacob (age ten) helps by putting away toys, rolling up rugs, and vacuuming the floor.

When you help out, you show God's love in a very practical way. You get to know other people and feel happy inside. So join in the body of Christ and help out!

God, Your plan is for us to help each other out. Thanks for reminding me to let other people know I'm willing to help. Show me what You would have me do for others. Amen.

A Heart That Serves

 id you know that a huge part of why Jesus came to earth was to serve others? Sounds kind of crazy, doesn't it? I mean, we're talking about *Jesus*, the Son of God! But it's true: "Even the Son of Man did not come to be served, but to serve, and to give his life as a ransom for many" (Mark 10:45).

Talk about powerful! And talk about a good motivation to start living *our* lives for others. If you want to be more like Jesus, develop a heart that serves. That includes doing your chores at home—preferably without being reminded ten times! Asking your teacher at school if there's anything she needs help with. Volunteering to join your dad at the church workday.

Finding opportunities to serve is pretty easy. And remember, Jesus came to earth to serve others. If that isn't motivation to have a heart that serves, I don't know what is!

Jesus, thank You for coming to earth to serve others—and to give Your life for us. With that as a model, I should be totally motivated to serve others and help out! Show me what You would have me do as I live my life for You. Amen.

When You Just Don't Want to Go

I hope you love going to church, but I understand that you might not always like going. Maybe the pastor is hard to understand or you just don't connect with the kids your age.

Ask God to help you understand how important it is to meet with other Christians and grow in the Lord. You can also pray to meet a new friend there—a brother in Christ, a friend, and a boy after God's own heart you can look forward to seeing each week.

Remember, you don't go to church mainly for the social time. You *do* go to worship Jesus. To learn more about Him. To bring other kids who need to know Jesus. And to serve others like Jesus did. When you don't want to go to church, remember that it isn't about you. It's about Jesus.

God, if church just isn't a lot of fun for me, help me
to have a change of heart. Worship is not about me—
it's about You. It's about learning more about You and
praising You and doing all I can for You. Remind me
of these things so I'll have a good attitude about going.
Amen.

Big Changes

Now is a really big time in your life. So many things are changing! Maybe you're transitioning from elementary school to middle school. Or you used to be the shortest kid in your class, but you had a huge growth spurt and are catching everyone else.

If you find things constantly changing in your life—your interests, your body, your dreams—don't freak out. The changes can seem overwhelming, but they're totally normal. And it helps to know that every boy your age is dealing with his own big changes.

When you do find yourself overwhelmed, don't hesitate to go straight to God and talk to Him about all your concerns. It's also good at this age to find an adult you trust—a parent or grandparent or a church leader—whom you can talk to when life gets totally complicated. And know that these big changes can bring great things!

Jesus, some changes in my life can be super confusing and overwhelming. I'm so glad that You stay the same and that You will always be there for me to talk to. Thank You for helping me deal with all the big changes in my life. Amen.

Not Ready for This

Some parts of growing up are tons of fun. Like being tall enough to go on all the scary rides at the amusement park. Or getting better at sports or music or whatever activity you love. Or transitioning from a smaller school to a bigger school with lots of new friends.

But some of this new growth can be puzzling and even scary as your body changes and your responsibilities increase—like having more chores around the house or way harder homework or staying home alone until your parents return from work. Sometimes you might feel as if you're not ready for all this.

Well, good news! No matter what is happening now, God's Word has the help you need to continue your journey through life with Jesus. His Word will help you discover who you are and who you're becoming as a guy after God's own heart. With His help, you've got this!

Lord, everyone says I should be excited about growing up and changing and getting older, but sometimes I just want to go back to being a kid! Thank You for Your Word, which has the answers I need for growing up and becoming like You. Amen.

The Right Start

How do you start your day? With a big bowl of your favorite cereal? A hot shower? Hurriedly throwing on your clothes and trying to make it to school on time?

The best way to start your day takes a minute or less. It's something you can do even if you have overslept or forgotten to study for your science quiz. You always start your day right when you get into the habit of thanking God each new morning for His love for you.

Do you realize there is never a minute in your life when you are not special to God and loved by Him? He made you. He knows everything about you. And He loves you—no matter what. So get your day off to a good start by telling Him, *Thanks for this day! And thanks for being with me as I make choices and learn things and do my best to live my life for You.*

God, mornings can be crazy! I tend to sleep in or forget stuff, but it only takes a minute to thank You for Your love and to ask for Your help throughout my day. And when I do this, things go so much better! Amen.

God Thinks You're Special

It's easy not to feel special when a sibling is getting more attention than you or a friend is having a lot of success. It's also easy not to feel special when your parents are super busy or stressed or when there's just a lot going on in life. At times like this, it helps to realize that no matter what's going on at home or at school, God loves you.

When you feel as if you're not very special—to yourself or to anyone else—you can know that you are a treasure to God and greatly loved by Him. When the kids at school aren't very friendly or nice, or when it gets pretty lonely, you can always count on God's love for you. This verse is so familiar, yet it's always so good to remember: "God so loved the world that he gave his one and only Son" (John 3:16). See how much He loves you?

Jesus, when I'm feeling less than special, I need to remember that You love me so much that You sent Your Son to die for me. That's how special I am! Thank You for surrounding me with Your love. Amen.

Never Alone

I f you've started staying home alone, you know what it's like to not have anybody around. Suddenly the house seems really big. And quiet. And, especially if it's dark outside, kind of creepy! Being alone can be fun—you can turn up your music, choose what to watch on TV, eat your favorite snack—but you probably wouldn't want to be alone *all* the time.

In the Bible, God tells us, "Never will I leave you; never will I forsake you" (Hebrews 13:5). This is such good news! God has promised never, ever to leave us alone.

Did you know that you can also feel alone in a crowd of people? It's true. You aren't sure whom to talk to or which group to walk up to. Even surrounded by people, you can feel alone. That's why it's so nice to know that Jesus is always there by your side. With Him, you're never alone.

Lord, sometimes it's nice to have time to myself, but at other times being alone is no fun at all—and actually kind of scary. Thank You for promising in Your Word never, ever to leave me. I'm glad You are always by my side. Amen.

Start Your Day Right

One time while I was reading my Bible, Psalm 118:24 (NKJV) really stood out to me. As I read it over and over and thought about it, I decided that before I even got out of bed each morning, I would begin each day with these words: "This is the day the LORD has made; we will rejoice and be glad in it."

You see, I had a bad habit. As soon as my alarm went off, I would start moaning and groaning and thinking, *Oh, no! Tell me it's not time to get up! Again? I'm so tired. Someone give me a break!*

But then I started acting on my decision to greet each new day with joy. I would say these words no matter what I was facing that day. Every morning, I started my day by reminding myself that because God was in charge of my day, I could be happy.

Jesus, it's tough to have a joyful attitude when I'm sick or stressed about school. But You have told us to rejoice and be glad every day, so that's what I'm determined to do! Thank You for giving me Your joy and Your happiness. Amen.

When You Feel like a Loser

Believe it or not, every boy has days when he feels like a loser. When he feels like he isn't as smart as the rest of the kids. When he feels like he isn't any good at sports. When he wonders if anyone will hang out with him during lunch and recess.

When I was a boy, I went through a period when I believed I was dumb at math. And when I sometimes struggled to write a full sentence that was correct, I just *knew* I was the only one who didn't get it. But my faith in Jesus and His love for me helped me overcome all the times I felt like I was a loser and not as good as everyone else. I knew deep in my heart that God had made me exactly the way I was and had created me for a purpose. Remember, God never makes mistakes, and He only makes winners!

God, sometimes it's easy to feel like a total loser! But I know deep down that I'm not because I'm made in Your image. Thank You for building me up when I'm down and showing me all the positive things about myself. Amen.

No Worries

When I was a kid, I dreaded a lot of things. Like giving the wrong answer when the teacher called on me. Like taking the Friday spelling test. And there was stuff outside of school that I super dreaded—like my keyboard recitals. I loved music, and I even liked practicing and playing the keyboard. But the recitals were 100 percent pure dread.

Do you know what helped me through the hard things in my days? Psalm 118:24 (NKJV)! No matter what I was worried about, remembering that "this is the day the LORD has made" helped me to follow through on the rest of the verse: I will "rejoice and be glad in it." That's what made the difference when things got tough.

It's fine to worry a little bit. Worry can sometimes be motivating. But God doesn't want you to freak out so much that you panic. If you're at that point, hand your dread over to Him. No worries!

Lord, sometimes the list of things I'm dreading totally starts adding up. From school to sports to stuff I need to do at home, help me to hand my worries over to You. Thank You that I can rejoice and be glad in all circumstances. Amen.

My Reflection

Most guys would never admit that they occasionally check the mirror. But you probably *do* look in the mirror—at least a few times a day, right? And here's a more important question: What do you see when you look at yourself in a mirror? Most guys immediately see everything that's wrong with them—or what they *think* is wrong with them. They pass right by their good features and never even stop to notice! Instead, their eyes go straight to every blemish, every strand of hair that won't cooperate, or too many freckles.

You can't escape mirrors, but they do have a purpose. You can use them to make sure your appearance is neat, which sends the message that you are a boy after God's own heart—that you are honest, reliable, innocent...that you have a good attitude. Once you see that reflection, go ahead and move on. The mirror has served its purpose!

God, as I get older, I care a little more about what I look like. Sometimes when I look at my reflection, I only see what's wrong with me instead of what's right with me. Help me to focus on my heart and my attitude. Amen.

What's Inside Counts

What if you could see right into your body and look at all the stuff inside? Or what if you could see into your heart and your mind? Actually, those are the main things God sees when He looks at you. The Bible says, "The LORD does not look at the things people look at. People look at the outward appearance, but the LORD looks at the heart" (1 Samuel 16:7).

Isn't that insane—and actually pretty cool? God doesn't care that you have teeth that stick out or if you haven't washed your hair in a few days. He's more concerned with your inward appearance. He's more interested in your heart and your character than your looks. That's so great to know in a world that tends to judge people according to how they look and what they own. If your heart and your mind are tuned toward Jesus, God is going to like what He sees.

Lord, it's nice to know that You're more concerned with my inside appearance than how I look on the outside. Help me to be like You—not judging other people on their outward appearance, but looking inside and getting to know people for who they really are. Amen.

Priceless

If you're going to spend time thinking about yourself, think about this: In God and through Jesus, you are the object of His love. You are a trophy of His grace. If you have accepted Jesus as your Savior, you are a member of God's family. *This* is who you really are!

God's opinion of you is the one that counts the most, not the opinion of your friends or your teachers or your siblings. Sure, it would be nice for everyone to think you're awesome, but that's not always going to happen. You're going to make mistakes, and other people are going to make mistakes. But no matter how many mistakes you make, you will always be priceless to God. And that's why we can pray this verse with confidence: "I praise you because I am fearfully and wonderfully made; your works are wonderful" (Psalm 139:14). You are one of God's works, and you are wonderful. That's the only opinion that really counts!

God, it's easy to let another person's opinion of me influence the way I feel about myself. In Your Word, though, You tell me that I'm priceless—that I'm "fearfully and wonderfully made." Please keep reminding me how valuable I am to You. Amen.

Build Yourself Up

Why is it that we keep thinking of ourselves negatively when God is constantly telling us how amazing we are in His eyes? And why are we so hard on ourselves when God went to such great lengths—including the death of His Son Jesus on the cross—to shout out and show His love for us? That makes no sense at all, does it?

If God is constantly expressing how pleased He is with us, we need to stop tearing down ourselves (and each other) and start building up ourselves (and each other)! When God speaks about us in His Word, He uses words like "love," "joy," and "priceless." Those are all such positive things.

So the next time you find yourself wanting to say something negative about yourself, ask, *Would God say this about me?* And then tell yourself that you're awesome in His eyes!

Jesus, it's pretty natural to want to put ourselves down. But that's not the way You talk about us in Your Word. Fill me up with Your love and Your confidence so I can speak words of kindness and truth.
Amen.

When I Mess Up

Life has pretty much guaranteed that we're going to mess up sometimes. We'll act unkind to someone, or we'll pay too much attention to what the "in guys" are wearing or how they're acting. And sometimes we get moody and pouty when things don't go our way. When these things happen, there are some things you can remember.

- You are "fearfully and wonderfully made"—exactly the way you are. God Himself made you, and He never makes a mistake!

- You can be joyful every second of every day—no matter what's happening to you—because God is with you.

- You are in a constant state of change as you grow year by year. Some of these changes are new, so make sure you talk them over with your mom or dad.

- You are as special as a one-of-a-kind snowflake, one of God's truly marvelous works!

God, life isn't going to be perfect, and I'm not going to be perfect! When I'm having a bad day or a challenging week, help me remember all the wonderful things You have said to me in Your Word. I am so happy for Your encouragement! Amen.

Life Is Good

When you're walking with Jesus, life is good! Sometimes it's easy, and sometimes it's challenging. Sometimes it's boring, and sometimes it's super busy. Sometimes it's happy, and sometimes it's sad. But when you're with Jesus, life is always good.

So make a decision to enjoy your journey with Jesus as you grow "in wisdom and stature, and in favor with God and man," just like He did (Luke 2:52). As you learn more about the Lord by reading your Bible, praying, and attending church activities, you'll also learn tons of lessons about life, other people, and yourself.

Walking with Jesus is way more exciting than climbing Mount Everest or rafting down the wildest rapids. It takes determination, endurance, and courage to live your life as a boy after God's own heart. It's the hardest thing you'll ever do—and the most rewarding. I'm so glad you're on this journey. Life is good when you're living for the Lord!

Jesus, help me remember the great things I've learned about Your love for me and the many ways You are working in my life. Life is always good because of You! Amen.

When You Forget

Have you ever fallen into bed dog-tired and then remembered, *Oops! I was supposed to spend time with Jesus today!* Maybe your parents or your Sunday school teacher challenged you to take a few minutes each day to read the Bible and pray, and you've been trying, but...

God understands when you forget to spend time with Him. He knows you're busy with school and friends and activities. But He also knows that all those things will go much better if you spend time talking to Him and reading His Word. Because really, your walk with God is the main point of this thing we call life.

So do something today to remind yourself to spend time with Jesus. Put a sticky note on your bathroom mirror. Set your Bible right beside your alarm clock. Make it a priority to spend time with God, because He's always willing to spend time with you.

Lord, it's easy to say "I'll do it tomorrow" to so many things—even the most important thing, which is spending time with You. Help me remember to spend some time reading Your Word and talking to You every day. Amen.

Time Wasters

Why is it so easy to spend time on things that aren't important and not on the things we should be doing? When you add up all the minutes of time you waste, you might be pretty amazed at the number!

It's important to take breaks and have some down time, but be careful that you're not just wasting time. Spending 30 minutes playing a game with your sister is something you'll remember way more than half an hour of zoning out with a computer game. An hour spent hiking with your mom is a much better use of your free time than an hour spent watching a movie you've already seen a million times. When you find yourself wasting time, ask God to help you make better use of your days and hours. He has some pretty great stuff planned for you, and you'll discover it when you use your time well!

God, our world makes it pretty easy for us to waste time. With TV and electronic games, I could spend hours doing basically nothing at all. Help me to make good use of my time and to spend it doing things for and with other people and You. Amen.

Time Is a Treasure

You would never throw away treasures like money or gold or silver, would you? And, as a boy after God's own heart, you shouldn't throw away your days and minutes either. Why? Because they too are riches and treasures! God says it is wise to realize how valuable time is. "Teach us to number our days, that we may gain a heart of wisdom" (Psalm 90:12). Today is a treasure God has handed to you to spend and use wisely.

So what will you do with today? Will you help a friend? Will you do something with your brother and sister and make a memory that lasts? Most of all, will you spend time with the Lord? Your time is a treasure. Use it wisely!

Jesus, sometimes it doesn't seem like I have very much—my favorite shirts are dirty or my family needs to go grocery shopping or I don't have cool electronics like my friends. But You've given me the treasure of time. Help me to use it wisely for You. Amen.

Do It Now

Do you have a habit of putting things off, especially things you don't want to do? Your mom tells you to clean up your room, but you tell yourself, *Oh, I'll just do it later.* And Your teacher has warned you about a big test coming up, and you still haven't cracked open the book.

News flash! Your messy room and that test aren't just going to go away. They'll be there staring you in the face tomorrow—even bigger and more imposing than they are today. So make a vow to do it now. Tackle the toughest thing first, whether it's your out-of-control closet or the test material you really need to learn. And promise yourself a reward when you're done—a few chocolate chip cookies, or maybe a trip to the park with your brother and your dog. Then get to work on the next thing. Soon enough, all the stuff will be checked off your list, and you'll be breathing a big sigh of relief.

Lord, it's easy to put stuff off until tomorrow. Help me stay motivated to get things done now instead of putting them off until later. Amen.

The Procrastination Problem

Do you know what it means to be a procrastinator? It means you're someone who says, "Oh, I can take care of that later. Right now I want to do something more fun!" Procrastinating—or putting stuff off—is one of those things that *seems* like no big deal. Until the moment arrives when you're supposed to have finished something. And then you hit the panic button!

Psalm 119:60 says, "I will hasten and not delay to obey your commands." God is pretty familiar with human nature. He made us, after all. And He knows our weak points. He also knows how to help us with those weak points.

When we delay doing something that needs to be done—and we hit the panic button—it's time to turn to Jesus. Ask Him to help you finish your task, and also ask Him to help you kick the habit of procrastinating. Once you get it done, then you can have fun!

Jesus, thank You for knowing me so well. Help me avoid procrastination as I become a guy after Your own heart. Show me what's important to get done, and then give me the motivation to do it. Amen.

A Time for Everything

Why is it that all the good stuff seems to happen at the same time? You want to play flag football *and* do karate, but the practices and classes happen at the same time. Your parents want you to choose one, but it seems impossible!

There's a verse in the Bible that says there is a time for you to do all those things you want and need to do that are truly important. "There is a time for everything, and a season for every activity" (Ecclesiastes 3:1). What God is saying here is that if He wants you to do it, He will help you find a way. Maybe you won't get to do it this month or this year, but He has a plan. And if it's in His plan, He'll find a way!

God, there are so many things I want to do and try.
But sometimes I don't have enough time, or my family doesn't have enough money to do these things.
Help me trust that You have the best plan ever for my life and that You will show me the things You want me to do. Amen.

Bored!

The opposite of having way too many things you want to do? Being bored, of course! Even if you're super busy, you can still have those awful moments of boredom.

Did you know that you need to watch out for the times when you *don't* have something to do? When you're desperate for something—anything—to do, you can be talked into doing stuff you aren't supposed to do. Even if you know those things are wrong. Certain friends can have a way of making something seem okay, and you need to be on the lookout for that. So after you've completed your schoolwork on time (a miracle!) and all your chores are done (another miracle!), have a list handy—at least in your mind—of some fun things to do that are totally okay. And banish boredom!

Lord, when I'm bored, it seems like I'm willing to do or play anything. Remind me that no matter what, I need to make good choices that honor You. Fill my mind and heart and life with positive activities that help me learn and grow. Amen.

Things I Want to Do Someday

D o you want to know the secret of never being bored? Make a list called "Things I Want to Do Someday." Include goals or dreams, hobbies, a series of books you'd like to read, or a new game or activity you want to learn.

This is where you put your free time to work! You can master a new skill or hobby. You can write and draw your own comic book adventure. You can go on a hike and put into practice some outdoor skills you've been learning. You can even work on a personal Bible study that's just for you. There are so many options!

It's easy to get stuck in the rut of playing games and watching shows. But I bet that pretty much nothing on your list of things you want to do someday is found on a computer screen or TV. So make your list, and the next time you're bored, use it as a source of inspiration.

Jesus, I know that You want me to grow up to be a guy after Your own heart. Help me to make a list of fun things that will help me become great in Your eyes. Amen.

Get Creative!

Think of all the things God created—the mountains, the sun and moon, the planets, the ocean, all of those animals, even the wide variety of people that populate our planet! It's pretty easy to see that our Creator is amazingly creative.

God made us to be creative too. And He made each of us with our own personal interests and talents and unique ways of looking at life. So tap into your creative side! You can pick up a new musical instrument and learn to play it. If you like to build things, see if you can help build something with your parents—maybe some new garden beds or even a chicken coop.

I'm so thankful that we have a creative God who made us creative too. He plans to grow something special in your life, so jump in and start making and discovering and learning stuff. And have fun!

Lord, You are such an amazing Creator! You made a big, wonderful world for me to explore, and You made me creative too. Help me use my gifts and talents to be creative for Your glory. Amen.

The Best Option

When you have so many things to choose from and so many ways to spend your time, how do you know what the *best* thing is to do? How can you use your time wisely and find out what your priorities are?

Many of your activities—like school, your chores at home, and going to church—are set in stone. They are not going to budge or change. But you get to choose the clubs you join, your activities with friends, and the way you spend your free time.

This is a great thing to talk to an older Christian about—how do you choose the best option? You can ask a parent or a church leader or an older sibling how they order their time and choose what to do. Ask them to pray that you will make good choices too, and then get going. You've got an awesome life to live!

God, as I get older, I find myself making more and more choices about what to do and whom to hang out with. Thank You that I can always turn to You about making the best choice. Amen.

All for Jesus

I have a little secret to getting things done. It's choosing to do it all for Jesus. The Bible says, "Whatever you do, whether in word or deed, do it all in the name of the Lord Jesus" (Colossians 3:17).

When I focus on doing everything for Jesus, it's amazing what happens. I'm able to think more clearly. I'm able to make better choices. I'm able to stay focused and on task. And as I'm working, I make sure I talk to Him! I ask for His help if I'm struggling, or I pray that I do my work to the best of my ability. Even if something doesn't turn out quite the way I wanted it to, I feel more at peace knowing I worked hard with a heart focused on Christ.

Lord, all You ask of us is that we do everything we do for You. When I remember this, it's easier to stay focused and work harder and be more determined. Help me to remember to live my life all for You. Amen.

Time for God

If you don't do some planning, time with Jesus can easily get crowded out of your life. Now, Jesus doesn't want you to neglect school, family, or other important activities. But just as you set aside time to go to school or practice a musical instrument, you need to set aside time to meet with God. After all, God is your number one priority.

So pick a time during the day when you will read His Word and pray. It really doesn't matter when and where, as long as you just do it. Throughout the day, remember to talk to Jesus. Tell Him "thank You" for the things He has given you. Ask for His help. And at night, read a little bit more in your Bible. Work on a devotional, maybe with a friend or sibling. Spend time with your family talking about the Lord. When you make time for God, He always shows up.

Jesus, spending time with You should be the most important thing I do every day. Help me get into the habit of reading Your Word and praying and learning more about You. Keep me on track as I choose to make time for You. Amen.

Seek Him

Kids play a lot of games that have to do with finding something. Easter egg hunts. Searching for buried treasure in the sandbox. And, of course, the old standby—hide and seek. In God's Word, He encourages us to seek Him:

- "Seek first his kingdom and his righteousness" (Matthew 6:33).

- "Blessed [happy] are those who keep his statutes and seek him with all their heart" (Psalm 119:2).

- "I seek you with all my heart" (Psalm 119:10).

- "You, God, are my God, earnestly I seek you" (Psalm 63:1).

The awesome thing is that He's right there waiting for you when you decide to seek Him. All you need to do is begin your search—by reading His Word, by attending church, by praying, or by listening to others talk about Him. He's well worth the search!

Lord, help me to look for You in the many ways and places where You show up. Wherever I seek You, I will find You. That's a game worth playing! Amen.

About Your Heart

I hope you're beginning to realize how important your time is, especially when it comes to time with Jesus. You make Jesus a priority when you make a commitment to spend time with Him...and follow through. Would you fail to show up for an appointment with a teacher? Would you skip a friend's birthday party? I don't think so! So why would you not make time for Jesus, the most important person in the world and in your life?

When you spend time with Jesus, great things happen. He gives you a happy heart. He helps you do your best and do it in a way that honors Him. And He does His amazing work of transforming you into what you really want to be—a boy after God's own heart. Then, when you put your head on your pillow each night, you can always thank Him for a wonderful day!

God, I want to pay better attention to how I spend my time. And most of all, I want to make sure I spend time with You each day. Thank You so much for transforming me into a boy after Your own heart. Amen.

J-E-S-U-S

The most important thing in your life is learning about Jesus and figuring out how you can be more like Him. That's why it's so important to read about His life in the Bible and to talk to Him. I use an *acrostic*—a word in which each letter stands for something—to remember some key truths about Jesus.

> **J**esus, the Son of God,
>
> **E**ntered the world as a baby and
>
> **S**acrificed Himself for sinners to
>
> **U**nite them with the Father by
>
> **S**ecuring eternal life for all who
>   believe in Him.

There's so much to learn about Jesus as you become more and more like Him!

Jesus, You are without a doubt the most important thing in my life! Thank You for entering this world as a baby and walking on this earth and dying on the cross for my sins. I love You! Amen.

A Different Kind of Growing

When you go to the doctor's office, it takes just two pieces of equipment to see how you've grown—a scale and a height chart. So how do you know you're growing in your walk with Jesus? You grow as you read your Bible, go to church, and surround yourself with friends who also love Jesus.

You grow in *wisdom* as you look in your Bible, pray, and talk with other Christians.

You grow in *God's grace* as God teaches you how to handle every problem.

You grow in *joy* as God blesses you with victories, accomplishments, and achievements you experience by His grace.

Lord, thank You for making me grow in so many different ways! Help me to continue growing into a boy after Your own heart. Amen.

Your Heart

Without your heart, you wouldn't be alive. And just as your physical heart is super important to your body, your spiritual heart is that important to your soul. The Bible talks a lot about the condition of the heart.

- "Above all else, guard your heart, for everything you do flows from it" (Proverbs 4:23).

- "A good man brings good things out of the good stored up in his heart, and an evil man brings evil things out of the evil stored up in his heart" (Luke 6:45).

So choose to fill your heart with good stuff! Are the music you listen to and the movies you watch and the games you play good for your heart? How about the books you read and the friends you hang out with and the activities you do? Make the choice to store good things in your heart and keep your heart healthy!

God, You talk a lot about our hearts in Your Word. Help me to store good things in my heart and to keep watch so that I can avoid anything evil. Amen.

Make It Count!

Life is a gift from God. On top of the life He has given you, He also has incredible plans and purposes for you as well. So make your life count! Because nothing could be worse than a life that counts for nothing. You have all the opportunities in the world to live an exciting life, to make a difference, to help others, and to live for God.

Be like an Army Ranger or a Navy SEAL who stands before his commanding officer—his CO—each day, ready to receive his orders, purpose, and direction. And be sure to get those marching orders from your CO—God! You do that by reading His Word, talking to Him, and being open to the plans He has for you. When you believe He's asking you to do something, obey His orders! Step out in faith and make your life count.

Jesus, I want to make my life count for something! I want to do amazing stuff and have awesome adventures just for You. Help me to obey Your orders and step out in faith. Amen.

Important Answers

You've arrived at that age where you're beginning to have a lot of questions about life. Here are some things you may have asked yourself: *What about my future? How can I find more good friends? Why do I keep doing the wrong thing? Is there a way I can get along better with my parents?*

There was a guy in the Bible who had a bunch of questions. Joshua was the man who became the general of God's army when Moses died. His job was to lead God's people into the Promised Land, and like every general and leader, Joshua wondered if he would be successful. So he talked to God about his worries, and God gave him a command to guarantee his success: "Be careful to obey all the law [the Bible] my servant Moses gave you...that you may be successful wherever you go" (Joshua 1:7).

God, thank You for wanting to bless me and for helping me to succeed. I can do this if I obey Your law. Help me to always seek answers in Your Word. Amen.

Dig In!

The best way to get to know God is by digging in to His Word.

Read your Bible. Start anywhere you like. The only wrong way to read the Bible is not to read at all.

Study your Bible. Ask your parents or youth leader to help you find some simple ways to get to know your Bible better.

Hear the Bible taught. Go to your youth group meetings and church to hear God's Word taught and explained so you can understand it—and, of course, choose to do what it says.

Memorize verses from the Bible. God tells us to meditate on the Bible. That means to think about His Word a lot so it's always in your heart.

Desire to spend time in God's Word. You already know the importance of eating physical food. Well, you need to see the spiritual food the Bible gives you as being important too...only more so!

Lord, thank You for giving me so many ways to get to know You through Your Word. Help me to get excited about reading and studying the Bible so I can learn a ton about You. Amen.

Living Forever

I once read a book about the adventures of Ponce de León. A legend says that he searched for a Fountain of Youth, believing that if he could find this fountain and drink some of its water, it would give him eternal youth. He would live forever as a young man.

You might not want to think about staying young forever. But you would probably like to live forever, right? The Bible tells us how that is possible—how you can live forever with Jesus in heaven. "The Holy Scriptures [the Bible]...are able to make you wise for salvation through faith in Jesus Christ" (2 Timothy 3:15).

God wants to give you eternal life, but there's just one problem: You need to be perfect, without sin. The good news? You have a Savior who can give you eternal life! Jesus is perfect. He is God. So choose to believe in Jesus. Through Him, you can live forever!

Jesus, I don't always make the right choices, so there's no way I can be perfect on my own. Thank You for giving me eternal life so I can live forever with You. Amen.

Prayer Warriors

Did you know the Bible is filled with stories about prayer warriors? From cover to cover—from Genesis to Revelation—the men who believed in God prayed to God. They prayed when there was trouble. They prayed when they worshipped. They prayed for people. They prayed while in battle. Whenever they needed strength or needed to make a decision, they turned to God and talked their situation over with Him.

And then there's the example of Jesus and the many times the Bible shows Him praying to God, His heavenly Father. I don't know about you, but I want to be a prayer warrior too. If Jesus and all these awesome heroes of the Bible relied so much on prayer, I want a piece of that action! I want to become a prayer warrior and learn to pray with courage when I'm faced with anything.

God, some people might think the Bible is boring, but it's filled with action and adventure, and its heroes are prayer warriors—men who believed in You and prayed to You. I'd like to become a prayer warrior too! Amen.

Join the Team

Prayer is sort of like being on a team. For instance, you are involved in the sport or project as a team, but there is a team leader or captain or coach or conductor. Someone is the leader. That leader is someone you can look to for help, listen to for advice, and follow because of that person's experience and knowledge.

When it comes to prayer, God is your spiritual leader. And the closer your relationship is to Him—the more you listen to what He says and then take action—the easier it is to talk to Him. You'll have an easier time figuring out what to say, and you'll feel close enough to Him to be comfortable in His presence. James 4:8 says, "Come near to God and he will come near to you." And Hebrews 10:22 says, "Draw near to God with a sincere heart."

God is your prayer leader—your coach, your captain. When you join His team and choose to follow His rules, it's easy to talk to Him.

Lord, I can't think of a better team leader than You!
Thank You for Your promise that as I get to know You,
I will have a deeper prayer life. Help me commit to
praying to You every single day. Amen.

Prayer Does Make a Difference

Have you ever prayed about something, but nothing seemed to happen, so you just kind of gave up? Or you might not quite understand the purpose of prayer and think, *What difference does prayer make anyway?* We think this way because we don't know about the many awesome promises God makes in the Bible about prayer and about answering our prayers. As a result, we don't think prayer makes any difference. So...we don't pray.

But God has promised us big things if we pray! The Bible says, "Ask and it will be given to you; seek and you will find; knock and the door will be opened to you" (Matthew 7:7). That's amazing stuff! Prayer *does* make a difference. It draws us closer to God and, through Him, gives us the power to make our lives better. So don't give up! Keep praying and talking to God and sharing your life with Him. You'll be so glad you did!

God, sometimes I feel like my prayers don't make a difference. But even if I can't see anything happening right away, reassure me that You are continuing to work in my life and in my heart as I keep praying. Amen.

Great Examples

The Bible is filled with examples of people who made the best choice—to pray about their life and their decisions.

King David praised God in prayer. As he faced super hard situations, he wrote, "I will exalt you, LORD, for you lifted me out of the depths and did not let my enemies gloat over me. LORD my God, I called to you for help, and you healed me" (Psalm 30:1-2).

Abraham prayed for his family. Abraham's relatives were living in another area. He couldn't talk to them or help them, but he could talk to God about them and pray for their safety (Genesis 18:20-33).

Jesus—wow! He was perfect and knew *everything* about prayer. This verse shows how important prayer was to Him: "Very early in the morning, while it was still dark, Jesus got up, left the house and went off to a solitary place, where he prayed" (Mark 1:35).

Jesus, when I don't know when or how to pray, lead me to Your Word. There I can find so many great examples of people who prayed when things were really hard. I want to talk to You in the same way! Amen.

The Real Thing

As you're on this adventure of living your life as a boy after God's own heart, make a commitment to be real. Be genuine. Be yourself. You don't need to try to impress others by saying and doing things you think will make them like you. It's tempting to act in a way that goes against God's Word to get friends or to be accepted by the "in crowd." But stop right there! The real you is the you who's trying to live for God. So be the real thing—and seek out the real thing.

Look for friends who aren't phony—who don't pretend to be someone they're not. For yourself, you should want to be the real thing, to be what God desires you to be—a godly young man. So be that person even if it means you won't be the most popular guy at school. At least you will be *you*. You will be the real thing. And God will be pleased with you.

Lord, when I'm tempted to be like everyone else, help me remember that You're the one I'm trying to please and impress. Help me to be genuine and real. Amen.

Tell the Truth

How would you feel if your parents or a good friend lied to you? That would hurt, wouldn't it? And it would also make it hard to trust anything else your parents or friends said to you. Lying hurts people. It damages family relationships and friendships. When you lie, it means you have something to hide or something you don't want other people to know about. Lies are like brick walls that keep people apart. They make it harder for you to share yourself openly with others.

Do you see how important it is to develop a habit of telling the truth? God says in His Word, "Let each one of you speak truth with his neighbor" (Ephesians 4:25 NKJV). The good news is that if you've fallen into the habit of lying, you can replace it with the habit of telling the truth. God will always help you be truthful because His Word is truth!

Jesus, sometimes it seems like no big deal to lie. But it's a really bad habit to develop, and it can ruin my friendships and family relationships. Help me to always speak words of truth. Amen.

Careful What You Say

Once you say something bad to someone, you can never take it back. Even if you say you're sorry and you didn't mean it, nobody is going to forget what happened. When you say something bad, it's a sign that something is wrong in your heart. And it's not just you that sees it—other people and God do too.

The solution to this? Make sure you put God's Word into your heart. When you do this, what comes out of your mouth will be God's thoughts and God's words. Sure, you'll still need to be careful about what you say and think before you speak. But it will be easier to speak good words because you'll be tuned in to the best word of all—God's Word.

Lord, sometimes I really wish I could take back my mean words. They hurt other people, they make me look bad, and they disappoint You. Help me to put Your Word into my heart so I can speak words of truth and love. Amen.

Be Patient

Waiting can be sooooo hard! Waiting for your birthday or Christmas. Waiting for your sister to get ready for church. Waiting for the rain to stop so you can go outside and play. Waiting doesn't come easily to most of us. But God asks us to wait. He asks us to be patient.

Sometimes, being patient means doing nothing. It's doing nothing instead of getting angry when kids make fun of you at school. It's doing nothing instead of getting even. The Bible says, "Be patient, bearing with one another in love" (Ephesians 4:2).

God is willing to give you patience whenever you ask for it. So go ahead and ask! And then learn to wait and listen for God's answer about how to respond the next time you don't get what you want or someone upsets you. Be patient!

God, waiting is really hard for me. I want stuff to happen right now, or I want to respond to a situation immediately. But You ask us to be patient. Help me to learn to wait when I need to. Amen.

Ignore Insults

Don't you just hate it when someone calls you a name or makes fun of you? What is your first reaction? You want to give an insult right back, don't you? He called you a name, so you immediately want to call him a name! Well, patience also applies to the insults you receive.

Proverbs 19:11 says that to be patient is to be wise: "A person's wisdom yields [produces] patience; it is to one's glory to overlook an offense." When someone insults you or makes you mad, try counting to ten before you say or do anything. This trains you to wait—to patiently do nothing until you are calm enough to say or do the right thing. It keeps you from losing your temper or hurting someone physically or with your words.

Remember, you're representing Jesus! And Jesus was incredibly patient and wise. He'll give you the same strength if you just ask Him.

Lord, when someone is super rude to me, I want to respond right away. But that response isn't usually the best response. Help me to be patient and wise and to wait before I say or do anything. Amen.

What Jesus Did

No one has ever experienced as much abuse as Jesus did. And He was perfect—totally undeserving of all the horrible things that happened to Him. Of course it's hard not to get angry and upset when someone picks on you and hurts you physically. But Jesus suffered far more hurt than we ever will.

When His enemies were calling Him names and taunting Him, what did He do? "When they hurled their insults at him, he did not retaliate; when he suffered, he made no threats. Instead, he entrusted himself to him who judged justly" (1 Peter 2:23). Wow! No retaliation. No threats. No, "Hey, I'm the Son of God. You're going to pay for this!" None of that. He continued to show patience and love to the very end. And when those soldiers nailed Him to the cross, Jesus prayed, "Father, forgive them, for they do not know what they are doing" (Luke 23:34).

Ultimate forgiveness and love!

Jesus, it's pretty unbelievable to see how You responded when You were being abused and tortured. You continued to show love, and You immediately forgave. Help me to use Your example in my own life.
Amen.

Crossroads

o you know what a crossroad is? It's a point in time when a choice must be made. I'm sure you've been with your parents in the car while on a vacation. There you all were, just driving along, and then the car stopped because you came to a place where several roads met. Well, that is a crossroad. You could continue to go straight, or you could turn right or left. There were three choices, and that crossroad forced your parents to make a decision.

We have a lot of crossroads in our lives. When you come to each one, it's easiest to make the right decision if you have a happy heart and a positive attitude. Most of all, you'll make the right decision which way to go when you are walking with Jesus and connected to Him. When you're following Jesus' directions, He will always make clear the way to go.

Lord, help me to stay connected to You so I can always make the right decision when I reach a crossroad in my life. Thank You that You have promised to guide my steps. Life is so much easier when I'm walking with You! Amen.

Choose Joy

There's a difference between happiness and joy, between being happy and being joyful. To begin, happiness is a feeling. Being happy comes as a result of something awesome happening in your life. When you get to do what you want, you're happy. And when you don't get to do what you want, you're unhappy.

Being happy is also what you experience when you're around happy, pleasant things or people you like. But joy comes from following Jesus' example. The joy of Jesus comes from within the heart and does not require happy things to be going on around you.

If you're following Jesus' example, you will want to show joy at all times, even when things aren't the way you want them to be. When your parents say they want you to have a happy heart, what they are really asking is that you have a joyful heart. A joyful heart is a heart that has joy no matter what is happening around you.

God, help me to see the difference between happiness and joy. And help me always to have a joyful heart, no matter what's going on in my life. When I choose You, I choose joy. Amen.

Knowing Christ

Even if you've been attending church or Christian school all your life, you might not be sure you have a personal relationship with Christ. If that's the case, ask yourself these questions: *What does it mean to be a Christian? Am I a Christian? And how can I become a Christian?*

These verses from the book of Romans tell you how you can become God's child:

- Romans 3:23 tells you about your sinful condition.

- Romans 6:23 shows you the result of your sinful condition and reveals the gift God offers to you instead.

- Romans 5:8 points out God's grace and love for you and Christ's answer to your sinful condition.

- Romans 10:9-10 reveals how to become a Christian.

Is this something you are wondering? You become a Christian by receiving Jesus Christ as your personal Savior. These verses from the book of Romans show you how.

God, I want to know Christ. I want to make sure I am a Christian. Please place people in my life who will help me come to know You and grow in You. And speak to me through Your Word. Amen.

You Did It!

Give yourself a high five—you've read this book all the way through! As you think back on all you've experienced and learned and prayed about since starting this devotional, I'm sure you can think of tons of ways you've gotten closer to God. I hope you'll go through this book again and again as you continue on your journey to becoming a boy after God's own heart.

But even more important than rereading these devotions is making the effort to put the things you've learned into practice. After all, practice makes permanent! My prayer is that you'll keep looking to Jesus, talking to God, growing in His ways, and receiving His joy. And as you do, you'll continue to receive His blessings!

Lord, may I spend time every day thinking about You, following Your Word, and being excited about Your work in my life. Help me to love You more, understand You better, and give my life to You completely. Thank You for teaching me more and more about becoming a boy after Your own heart. Amen.

More Books by Jim George

A Boy After God's Own Heart

Jim George helps you understand why God is important in everything you do. He teaches what the Bible says about parents, making right choices, choosing good friends, taking school seriously, and following after God.

A Boy's Guide to Discovering His Bible

As a boy growing up, do you know one of the most important things you can do is read your Bible? God has a lot to share with you. Get to know your Bible better—it's an amazing adventure!

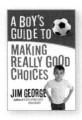

A Boy's Guide to Making Really Good Choices

How can you know you're doing the right thing? Jim George shows you how to think through your options, realize the possible consequences, and develop good decision-making skills.

You Always Have a Friend in Jesus for Boys

Athletes. Writers. Artists. Musicians. Actors. Role models. People you look up to. But the best role model of all? That's Jesus—the hero who's also your best friend. Explore ten character traits of Jesus that you can apply to your life every single day.

To learn more about Harvest House books and
to read sample chapters, visit our website:

www.harvesthousepublishers.com

HARVEST HOUSE PUBLISHERS
EUGENE, OREGON